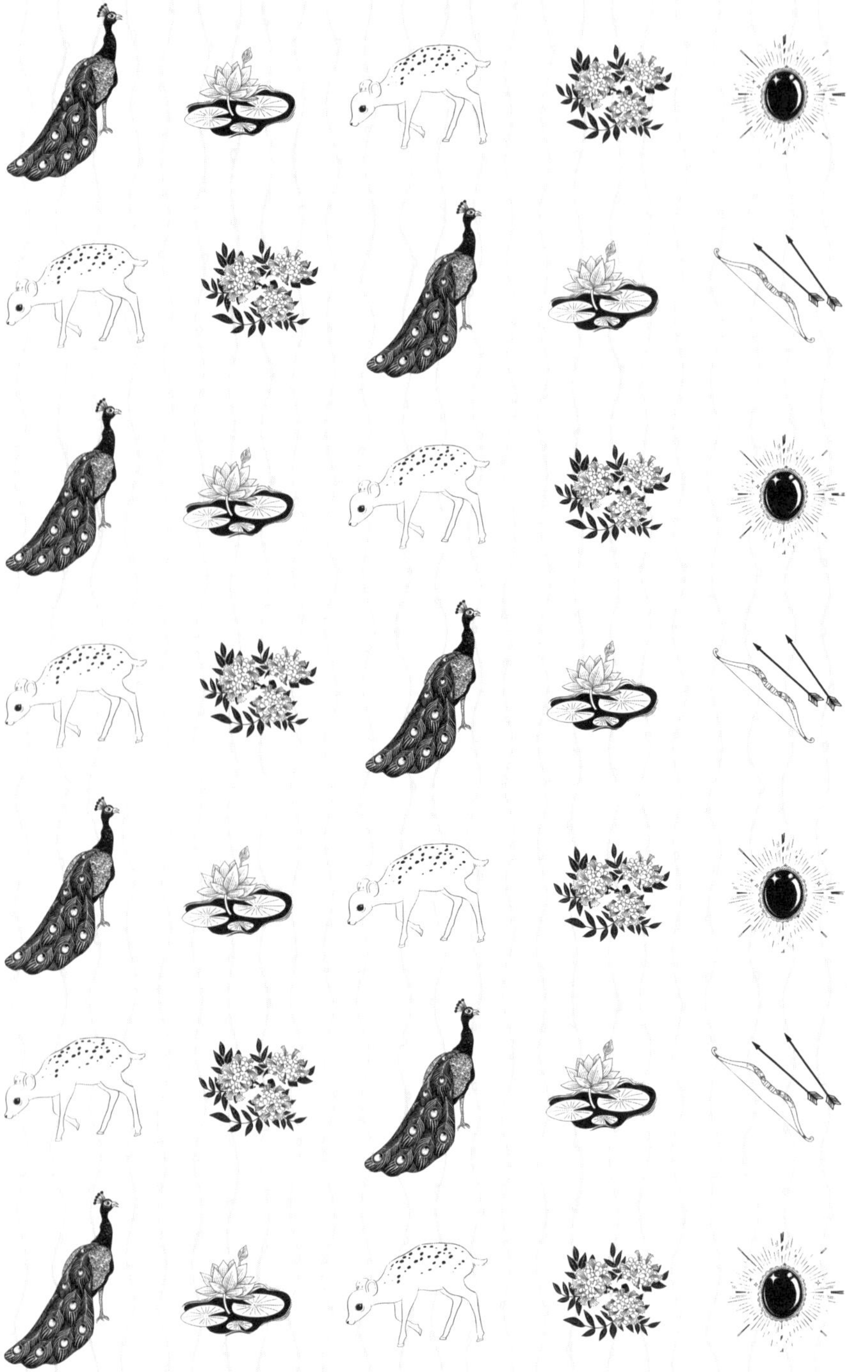

UNDER THE WISH-FULFILLING TREE

The Wondrous Worlds of Kalidasa

Rohini Chowdhury is an established literary translator and the author of more than 20 children's books. Her literary interests include mythology, folklore, mathematics, and history.

Her primary languages as a translator are pre-modern and modern Hindi, and English. Her translations include the seventeenth-century Braj Bhasha text *Ardhakathanak*, widely regarded as the first autobiography in an Indian language, as well as Tulsidas's *Ramcharitmanas*, the sixteenth-century retelling of the story of Rama, unanimously regarded as the greatest achievement of Hindi literature.

Rohini is also interested in the preservation of folk literature and traditional stories. She runs the story website www.longlongtimeago.com and co-authors *The Story Birds* on Substack.

She also writes *Eaten by a Fish*, a research-based publication on Indian literature, on Substack.

Born and educated in Kolkata, India, Rohini now lives and writes in the UK.

UNDER THE WISH-FULFILLING TREE

The Wondrous Worlds of Kalidasa

ROHINI CHOWDHURY

hachette INDIA

First published in hardback in 2025 by Hachette India
(Registered name: Hachette Book Publishing India Pvt. Ltd)
An Hachette UK company
www.hachetteindia.com

1

Illustrations by Priyanka Pachpande
Photograph of Meguti Jain Temple ruins on page 11 by Sarah Welch, sourced from Wikimedia Commons, under the Creative Commons CC0 1.0 Universal Public Domain Dedication.

Excerpts on pages 123–125 from *Vikramorvashiyam: Quest for Urvashi* and pages 193–195 from *Raghuvamsam: Line of Raghu*, both translated by A.N.D. Haksar and published with the kind permission of Penguin Random House India.

Other excerpts are in the public domain or are featured under Fair Use.

ISBN 978-93-5731-955-3

Hachette Book Publishing India Pvt. Ltd
4th & 5th Floors, Corporate Centre
Plot No. 94, Sector 44, Gurugram – 122003, India

Typeset by Manmohan Kumar, Delhi

Printed and bound in India
by Thomson Press India Ltd

MIX
Paper | Supporting responsible forestry
FSC www.fsc.org FSC® C010615

In memory of my mother,
who gave me natya, kavya, and Kalidasa.

Contents

The Poet and His Enchanted Pen

Many years ago, when I was a young girl, I heard the story of Shakuntala, the ascetic's daughter, and her ill-fated love for the brave King Dushyanta. I was completely drawn into the story, and followed Shakuntala's adventures with bated breath – her meeting and falling in love with the handsome stranger who turns out to be the king of the land, the sage's curse which makes the king forget her, and the tragic and disastrous loss of the king's signet ring, which had been her only means of breaking the curse. This tale, which Kalidasa tells with infinite beauty in his play *Abhijnanashakuntalam*, was my first introduction to the poet; ever since then, I have been a devoted admirer of his works.

I am not alone in my admiration. Kalidasa is universally regarded as classical Sanskrit's greatest poet and playwright, a status he has occupied from very early times and justified by the excellence and versatility of his works. For at least the last 1,500 years or so, his works have been performed, recited, read, translated, studied, and imitated across the

Indian subcontinent and, in more recent times, in other countries around the world. *Abhijnanashakuntalam*, in particular, has been globally hailed as the epitome of literary skill and achievement in any genre or language, while in India, scholars and Sanskritists have been unanimous in declaring his epic *Raghuvamsham* one of the greatest works of Sanskrit literature.

Poets after Kalidasa have acknowledged him as their master and admired him for the sweetness and unrivalled perfection of his verses. One such admirer was the seventh-century poet and writer Banabhatta, well known to us as the author of the romance *Kadambari*. Bana was also the court poet of King Harsha of Thaneshvar (reigned 606–647 CE) and composed *Harsha Charita* ('The Deeds of Harsha'), a biography of the king. He was familiar with the works of Kalidasa and praises him in *Harsha Charita*. He writes: 'Who would not feel delight when Kalidasa's perfect sayings, charming with sweet sentiments like honey-laden flowers, come forth?'*

The twelfth-century poet Jayadeva, author of the *Gita Govinda*, calls Kalidasa 'Kavikulguru' or 'lord of poets', and, some 200 years later, the commentator Appaya Dikshita (c. 1305–1405 CE) of Vijayanagara applauds him as the foremost of all ancient poets. Others, such as the philosopher Kumarila Bhatta (590–650 CE), quote admiringly from his works in their writings. Some poets, such as Vatsabhatti, the author of the Mandsaur Silk Weaver's inscription of 437 CE, unashamedly imitate his poetry, or, like Ravikirti, the author of the Aihole inscription of 634 CE, in a bid for greatness,

*Translation based on M.R. Kale's translation in his introduction to Kalidasa's *Raghuvamsham*, in *The Raghuvamsa of Kalidasa*, p. viii.

compare themselves to him. (We learn more about these inscriptions below.)

In the last 200 years, Kalidasa's works also achieved fame and popularity outside India. He was introduced to Europe and the English-speaking world in 1789, when Sir William Jones, orientalist and founder of the Asiatic Society of Bengal, translated his play *Abhijnanashakuntalam* into English. The translation, titled *Sacontalá or The Fatal Ring*, was received with great enthusiasm from the leading scholars and poets of the day, including the German poet and polymath Goethe. The play was rapidly retranslated into German and French. With this, Kalidasa's fame spread rapidly throughout Europe and North America. Over the next hundred years, his works, particularly *Abhijnanashakuntalam*, were translated and retranslated into English and several other European languages. By the beginning of the twentieth century, Kalidasa's fame as classical India's greatest poet and playwright had been firmly established.

Kalidasa's Life and Times

So, who then was Kalidasa?

Despite his importance in the world of literature, we know practically nothing about the poet himself. We do not have any contemporary record about him, whether historical, epigraphical, or manuscript. Nor does he give us any details about himself in his works – when and where he was born, where he spent his creative years, who his family or friends were, or the other poets and writers with whom he must have interacted.

The 'Servant of Time'

He does not give us even his real name. His epics and lyric poems have no name attached to them; we know only through later sources that he has written them. In the prologues to his plays, he refers to himself only as 'Kalidasa', which means 'the servant or devotee of the goddess Kali'. Kali, as the fiercest form of Durga or Devi, the Supreme Goddess, is associated with the opposing forces of destruction and creation. She is also time (kala) in the feminine, and in that form, the constant creator. Therefore, the name Kalidasa may also be translated to mean 'the servant of time' or 'the servant of creative power'. It was probably assumed by the poet to emphasize his devotion to the creative principle; it is unlikely that this was his real name.

Popular Legends and Fanciful Tales

This absence of information and the poet's enduring celebrity status across the centuries inevitably gave rise to several tales and legends about him. Several of these stories say that he was orphaned at a very young age, that he was a devotee of Kali and acquired the gift of poetry by her grace. Another relates how the poet, though an unlettered fool at the time, was married to the wise and learned Princess Vidyottama of Ujjayini; upon discovering that the man she had married was illiterate and devoid of all learning, the princess banished him from the palace. He then wandered the world in search of knowledge; finally, in return for his unstinting devotion, the goddess Kali endowed him with learning, and he returned to his wife as the greatest poet of all time.

A Sri Lankan tradition makes him a friend of the poet Kumaradasa, who is often identified with King Kumaradhatusena (reigned 515–524 CE) of Anuradhapura. According to legend, Kalidasa was murdered by a courtesan while on a visit to meet Kumaradasa. Overcome with grief, Kumaradasa ended his own life by throwing himself upon Kalidasa's funeral pyre. However, none of these tales have any historical basis.

More such stories about Kalidasa are found in the sixteenth-century *Bhojaprabandha*, a fictionalized account of the life of King Bhoja of Malwa (reigned c. 1010–1055 CE), by a poet called Ballala. Ballala makes Kalidasa a favourite of the king and, along with other well-known Sanskrit poets (such as Bhavabhuti and Dandin), one of the nine literary jewels that graced his court. Modern research has shown that Kalidasa lived at least four centuries before Bhoja, and the poets depicted as contemporaries in the stories were separated from each other by hundreds of years. This clearly shows that the stories of the *Bhojaprabandha* are only fanciful tales with no basis in fact.

What the Scholars Say

Since Kalidasa has told us nothing about himself, and we have no reliable information from other contemporary sources, scholars have resorted to searching his works for words, expressions, and references that hint at some aspect of his life and times. They have also looked at later sources, viz., the works of later poets and writers that quote or refer to his poems and plays, the commentaries on his works by critics and scholars, and the handful of inscriptions that mention him or his works. Based on their analyses of these sources, different scholars have put forward different theories about the poet, his life, and his works.

Finding the Land of His Birth

We do not know where Kalidasa was born or where he may have spent his early years. Scholars have suggested various places across the subcontinent as the place of his birth. These suggestions, which include regions as diverse as Nepal and the modern Indian states of Jammu and Kashmir, West Bengal, Bihar, and Maharashtra, are mostly based on the poet's descriptions of a place or region and remain unconvincing.

Tradition points to Malwa (the ancient kingdom of Avanti) in west-central India as the land of his birth but remains divided between the ancient cities of Dhara and Ujjayini. Kalidasa describes this region in loving detail in his poems *Ritusamharam* and *Meghadutam*. His descriptions of Ujjayini in the latter are particularly vivid. He describes the city in detail – her mansions and terraced palaces, her flower-filled gardens, the refreshing breeze from the River Shipra at dawn, carrying upon it the scent of lotuses and the 'love-maddened' cries of sarus cranes. He writes of the temple to Mahakala (Shiva as Cosmic Time) set among gardens cooled by river breezes, where, as dusk falls, the evening rituals commence. The Mahakala temple was an important landmark in Ujjayini in ancient times (it was destroyed by Iltutmish, the Sultan of Delhi, in 1235 CE).

From Kalidasa's descriptions, it is clear that Ujjayini was a city he knew well, and one that he loved and admired. Given this, it could be true that Kalidasa belonged to this region, and that Ujjayini was where he was born and raised. But we have no evidence other than his descriptions to confirm this theory. So, at least for now, his place of birth must remain unknown.

Ujjayini: His Creative Home?

Kalidasa's intimate descriptions of Ujjayini suggest that he spent at least some part of his creative life there. The city was the bright and bustling administrative capital of the ancient kingdom of Avanti. Centuries of stable rule under powerful and able kings had made the city wealthy and prosperous. It lay at the junction of two important trade routes which connected it to cities and ports within India and, across land and sea, to cities and ports in lands as far away as ancient Egypt, Rome, and the Mediterranean. This made Ujjayini an important centre for trade and a meeting place for travellers from across the ancient world. The city thus grew into a vibrant cultural and intellectual hub where new ideas were freely exchanged, and new art forms thrived and grew. Its observatory, famously associated with the astronomer Varahamihira, was renowned throughout the ancient world. Time in ancient India was reckoned from the meridian that passed through Ujjayini – a fact which emphasized Ujjayini's strategically central location and its political, cultural, and economic importance in the subcontinent.

The city was also an early centre for Buddhism, and Jainism and the worship of Shiva were also well-established here. Many great Sanskrit dramas – such as the fifth-century *Mricchakatikam* (The Little Clay Cart) by Sudaraka, the story of Charudutt and his love for the courtesan Vasantasena – are set in Ujjayini. Others are centred around the life of Vasavadatta, daughter of King Pradyota of Ujjayini during the sixth century BCE; these include *Swapnavasavadattam*

(The Dream of Vasavadatta) by Bhasa, one of the earliest Sanskrit playwrights who lived and wrote sometime during the first or second century CE.

The city's wealth, its pluralism, and its vibrant cultural atmosphere attracted poets, writers, and thinkers from all over the world. It is not unlikely that Kalidasa was one of them. From his writings, it is evident that he was familiar with court life and that he himself lived an affluent and comfortable life. He was a follower of Shiva – for instance, he begins all his plays with an invocation to the god – but broadminded and inclusive in his beliefs, for he honours other gods and faiths as well in his writings. He was familiar with the Vedas and the Upanishads and well versed in Vedantic thought and tradition and in the dualistic principles of the Samkhya and Yoga systems of philosophy. He was also familiar with the Puranas, the *Ramayana* and the *Mahabharata*, and the *Bhagavad Gita*. His detailed descriptions of places and landscapes show that he had travelled widely across India and was a keen and accurate observer of the places he visited and saw.

Kalidasa's Date

Kalidasa's chronology is one of the enduring puzzles of Indian history – we do not know when he was born or when he died. It has also been impossible to date his works with any precision. It is customary for poets to mention their patrons (sometimes more than once!) in their works, praising them for their wisdom, generosity, and other good qualities. But Kalidasa is as silent about his patron as he is about himself. Nor can his writings be definitively related to any specific period in history, for he drew evenly on history, mythology, the epics, and even folk and fairy lore for his settings and plots.

Scholars have analysed his works in minute detail, searched for parallels in history, examined inscriptions and the works of other writers, and even looked for clues in sculpture and art in an attempt to determine the time in which he lived and wrote. Some have tried to compute his dates on the basis of astronomical events (such as a lunar eclipse in *Abhijnanashakuntalam*) mentioned in his works. Different scholars have put forward different dates for the poet, spanning several hundred years. V.V. Mirashi and N.R. Navlekar discuss the various theories in their book *Kālidāsa: Date, Life and Works* (1969). I have drawn extensively from their book in writing this section.

The Shunga Theory

The earliest date that is assigned to Kalidasa is c. 150 BCE, during the reign of the Shunga king Agnimitra (reigned c. 149–141 BCE), who is also the hero of his play *Malavikagnimitram*. The play is set in Vidisha, capital of the Shunga kings during Agnimitra's rule, and though it is mainly a product of the poet's imagination, refers to some historical events that took place during Agnimitra's rule. However, this date is unsupported by external evidence, and the arguments based on the internal evidence of the play are regarded as unconvincing by many scholars.

The Aihole Inscription

The latest possible date for Kalidasa is given by the Aihole inscription, which is dated to 634–635 CE. The language of the inscription is Sanskrit and the text consists of 37 verses in praise of emperor Pulakeshin II, the greatest of the Chalukyan kings, who ruled the Deccan from 610 to 642 CE. The eulogy to the emperor is inscribed on a block of stone set in a sidewall of the Meguti Jain temple in Aihole, Karnataka.

The Aihole inscription has been translated by various scholars, including the German Indologist Franz Kielhorn. Kielhorn gives his translation and a detailed description of the inscription in his article 'Aihole Inscription of Pulikesin II; Saka-Samvat 556' in the 1900–01 issue of *Epigraphia Indica*.

The author of the inscription calls himself Ravikirti. After acknowledging the gifts he has received from his patron, Pulakeshin II, he launches into an account of the Chalukya dynasty and lauds the might and glory of Pulakeshin II. In Verse 37, he states that he built the temple with the support of his patron, the emperor. He also declares that he is the author of the eulogy, and who 'by his poetic skill has attained to the fame of Kalidasa and of Bharavi'. Bharavi is a celebrated Sanskrit poet who lived sometime during the sixth century CE; he is the author of the epic *Kiratarjuniya* (Of Kirata and Arjuna). While Ravikirti is not quite equal to either of the poets he mentions, according to Kielhorn he is an accomplished poet, conversant with the rules and conventions of writing praise poetry. He is also clearly familiar with the works of Kalidasa and Bharavi, and has drawn inspiration from both the *Raghuvamsham* and the *Kiratarjuniya*. Kielhorn demonstrates Ravikirti's reliance on the works of both poets with examples. Kielhorn adds that while describing the deeds of his patron in Verses 17–32, Ravikirti takes as his model Canto 4 of the *Raghuvamsham* in which Kalidasa describes the conquests of King Raghu.

AN ARCHIVAL PHOTO OF THE MEGUTI JAIN TEMPLE IN AIHOLE, KARNATAKA, WHERE THE AIHOLE INSCRIPTION CAN BE SEEN

Kielhorn's findings are accepted by most scholars. It is thus generally agreed that the Aihole inscription proves without a doubt that Kalidasa (and Bharavi) lived before 634 CE, and that this is the latest date that may be assigned to Kalidasa.

It is also generally accepted that by about 600 CE, Kalidasa's fame was well-established and his *Raghuvamsham* well-known across India. Another Chalukyan inscription of interest is the Mahakuta pillar inscription of Mangalesh, son and successor of Pulakeshin II. The inscription, dated to 602 CE, consists of sixteen lines in praise of the Chalukyan dynasty. As Kielhorn points out, the writer of the inscription has, in his eulogy, actually copied half a verse from Canto 1 of the *Raghuvamsham*!

Inscriptions dated before the Chalukyan ones also borrow or imitate verses from Kalidasa's works. According to Kielhorn, the Bodh Gaya inscription of Mahanaman, which is dated 586–587 CE and records the construction of a Buddhist temple in Bodh Gaya by the Sri Lankan monk Mahanaman, was inspired by a verse from Canto 12 of *Raghuvamsham*. Kielhorn has also drawn attention to the fact that a verse from Canto 6 of Kalidasa's epic has been imitated in one of the Nagarjuni Hills cave inscriptions of the Maukhari king Anantavarman; these inscriptions are dated c. 550 CE or earlier.

The Mandsaur Silk Weavers' Inscription

Several inscriptions of the Aulikar kings, who ruled Malwa from the fourth to the sixth centuries CE, have been found in Mandsaur in Madhya Pradesh, the site of the ancient city of Dashapura. Among these, of special interest to us is an inscription known as the inscription of the Silk Weavers. Former professor of archaeology K.L. Mankodi discusses this in detail in his paper, 'The Mandasor Silk Weavers' Inscription of 437 CE and the Temples of the Aulikars'.

The inscription, says Mankodi, gives us the following information: In the year 437 CE, the Gupta emperor Kumaragupta ruled in Magadha, while the Aulikar king Bandhuvarman ruled in Dashapura in western Malwa. In the same year, a guild of silk weavers from Gujarat, who had earlier settled in Dashapura, built a temple to the sun god there. The building of this temple was supervised by one Vatsabhatti. Sometime during the next 37 years, the temple suffered structural damage. In 473 CE, the same silk-weavers' guild had it repaired, once again under the supervision of Vatsabhatti, who also composed the inscription in praise of the temple restoration.

Several scholars, including Mirashi and Navlekar, have demonstrated that Vatsabhatti's commemorative verses imitate verses and ideas from Kalidasa's *Meghadutam* and *Ritusamharam*. For instance, Vatsabhatti's description of the mansions of Dashapura, which he compares to white clouds, resembles Kalidasa's description of the lofty palaces of Alaka in *Meghadutam*, while his description of winter imitates Kalidasa's description of the season in *Ritusamharam*. Vatsabhatti's verses are not especially distinguished, and he says that he composed them 'with great effort'. Therefore, it is argued, it is more likely that Vatsabhatti, not Kalidasa, must have been the borrower – which indicates that Kalidasa must have composed his works before Vatsabhatti, that is, before 473 CE. This theory places Kalidasa approximately in the middle of the fifth century CE.

Vatsyayana's 'Kamasutra'

Mirashi and Navlekar also draw attention to Kalidasa's familiarity with the *Kamasutra* of Vatsyayana, a work upon which he has drawn several times in his poems and plays. Vatsyayana's great work, which deals with the nature of love, life, and relationships, has been dated to c. 330 CE. Given the depth and extensive scope of his work, it is unlikely that Vatsyayana would have drawn his ideas from a few scattered passages in Kalidasa's writings. It is much more likely that Kalidasa would have borrowed from Vatsyayana. If this is indeed true, Kalidasa must have lived after the composition of the *Kamasutra*, that is, after 330 CE.

If we accept the dates suggested by the Mandsaur Silk Weavers' inscription and by the similarity between some passages in Kalidasa and Vatsyayana, Kalidasa may be more precisely placed between 350 and 450 CE.

The Vikramaditya Tradition

A long-standing tradition maintains that Kalidasa was the court poet of a king who ruled from Ujjayini, who was a patron of the arts, who defeated the Shakas and assumed the title of 'Vikramaditya' or 'Sun of Valour'. This belief is supported by a surprising number of well-respected scholars in India. They suggest that the title of Kalidasa's play *Vikramorvashiyam* and the several occurrences of the word 'vikrama' within it obliquely honour his patron, King Vikramaditya; that his royal patron ruled from Ujjayini, they say, is self-evident from Kalidasa's glowing descriptions of the city.

The tradition identifies this king as the legendary Vikramaditya who ruled from Ujjayini in the first century BCE and drove the invading Shakas out of Malwa; he then established the Vikrama Era in 57 BCE to commemorate his victory over them. His valiant deeds have been told and retold in later story collections such as the eleventh-century *Kathasaritsagara* by Somadeva. The *Baital Pachisi* or *Vetalapanchavimsati* consists of 25 tales, still immensely popular in India, that relate the king's encounter with a vetala. Despite his place in story and legend, there is no evidence to prove that he was a real, historical person.

As Mirashi and Navlekar point out, even the era named after him was originally known as Krita; it became associated with him only as late as the tenth century CE. He is also sometimes identified as the Paramara king Vikramaditya, supposedly ruling from Ujjayini during the first century BCE. But there is no conclusive evidence of his reign or, indeed, of any king called Vikramaditya during that time.

'Vikramaditya' was a title often given to kings or assumed by them to commemorate their achievements in battle or as rulers. Several kings have borne this title in India's history, including kings who ruled at Ujjayini. Various scholars have identified one or other of these kings as Kalidasa's patron. The more important of the kings so identified include Gautamiputra Satakarni (reigned c. 106–130 CE), the greatest of the Satavahana emperors, and Yashodharman of Malwa (ruled 515–545 CE), a king of the Aulikar dynasty who defeated the powerful Huna king, Mihirakula. But there is no evidence to show that Kalidasa lived during the reign of either of these kings.

The Chandragupta II Connection

Modern scholars place Kalidasa during the Gupta period of India's history. Only one king called Vikramaditya is known to have ruled between 350 and 450 CE, the period suggested by the Mandsaur Silk Weavers' inscription and the composition of the *Kamasutra*. This was the Gupta emperor Chandragupta II, who ruled across northern India from c. 375 to 415 CE. He defeated the Shaka rulers of western India and took over their territories, extending the large empire he had inherited from his father, Samudragupta (ruled c. 335–375 CE), to include Malwa with its capital at Ujjayini. He then took the title 'Vikramaditya'. Gold coins from his reign are stamped with his name on one side and the title 'Sri Vikrama' or 'Vikramaditya' on the other. He also made Ujjayini the second capital of his empire. He encouraged learning and the arts and was himself an accomplished poet. Chandragupta II, therefore, also satisfies, quite neatly, the description of the Vikramaditya of tradition.

However, many scholars disregard this theory on the grounds that there is no evidence to definitively prove that Kalidasa lived between 350 and 450 CE, or that he was indeed the court poet of Chandragupta II.

Kalidasa's Works

Kalidasa's silence about himself led to a large number of works being attributed to him over time. The name 'Kalidasa' was also assumed by many other poets in Sanskrit literary history. This has made it even harder to identify the works of the 'real' Kalidasa.

Extant Works

Of the 40 or so works attributed to him over the centuries, modern scholarship accepts only seven as having been composed by him. These are:

- The two lyric poems: *Ritusamharam* (The Gathering of the Seasons) and *Meghadutam* (The Cloud Messenger);
- the three dramas: *Malavikagnimitram* (Malavika and Agnimitra), *Vikramorvashiyam* (Urvashi, Won by Valour), and *Abhijnanashakuntalam* (The Recognition of Shakuntala); and
- and the two epics: *Raghuvamsham* (The Lineage of Raghu) and *Kumarasambhavam* (The Birth of the War God).

An eighth work, *Kunteshvaradautyam* (Embassy to the Lord of the Kuntalas; also sometimes called *Kuntaleshvaradautyam*) is mentioned by the eleventh-century Kashmiri scholar Kshemendra in his *Auchityavicharacharcha*, a treatise on poetics, but no copy or manuscript of the work has yet been found.

Recensions and Manuscripts

We do not have Kalidasa's works as he wrote them. Instead, they have come to us in several recensions (different or revised versions of a text) from different parts of the country. We do not know exactly when or how these different versions came about. It is possible that after his death, changes were made to his works. We do not know who made these changes or why, but it is not unusual in Sanskrit literary history for later scholars and poets to make their own amendments and additions to a text.

Before the advent of printing, written texts were copied again and again as they were passed down through time, and mistakes in copying inevitably occurred, even in the case of the most careful scribes. Texts, as they were transmitted through the centuries or from one geographical region to another, were also often copied from one script into another. Each script has its particular features, its peculiarities and limitations, so that, in addition to mistakes in copying, changes in the text occurred due to the change in script. In this way, gradually, over time, words, sentences, and even entire passages in a text could change.

These processes were true for Kalidasa's writings as well, and in time, resulted in hundreds of manuscripts, belonging to one or other of the various recensions, of his poems and plays. Many of these manuscripts are available to us today. However, not only do the various recensions of a work differ from each other, but the manuscripts within a particular recension of that work also differ, sometimes significantly, from each other. The differences may lie in their length, or in the order and number of their verses. It is possible that Kalidasa's original manuscripts were written in a form of Brahmi; the manuscripts that we have today are in a variety of regional scripts such as Devanagari, Bengali, Grantha, Telugu, and Malayalam. All surviving manuscripts of Kalidasa's works date from after his lifetime.

Commentaries and Commentators

Over time, Kalidasa's works were also studied and analysed by critics and commentators across the country. Many of the commentaries written by them are available to us today and have contributed immeasurably to our knowledge and understanding of Kalidasa's works. The earliest known commentator on his works is the Kashmiri scholar Vallabhadeva, who probably lived during the early years of the tenth century CE. Vallabha has commented on Kalidasa's *Meghadutam*, *Raghuvamsham*, and *Kumarasambhavam*; his commentary, *Panjika*, was critically edited by E. Hultzsch in 1911. The Telugu poet and critic Mallinatha Suri, who lived probably during the latter half of the fourteenth century, is regarded as an authority on *Meghadutam*, *Raghuvamsham*, and *Kumarasambhavam*. His commentary, *Sanjivani*, though much later than many others, is popular for its clarity and erudition. Various readings of Kalidasa's works are also available from the commentaries.

As we saw earlier, many later writers refer to Kalidasa in their works, often quoting verses or passages from his poems and plays. Though such references are relatively few in number and the verses and passages quoted quite short, they do help in identifying his works and give us an appreciation of the esteem in which he was held.

Sanskrit Kavya

In Sanskrit poetics, the kavi is not just a poet – he is also a seer who looks beyond the ordinary and the mundane. His creative work, or kavya, is not restricted to poetry but includes all kinds of literary compositions, whether in prose or verse. Kavya is subdivided into two categories:

- Drishya: that which can be seen or exhibited; and
- Shravya: that which can only be heard or chanted.

Drishya kavya or drama is also termed natya. Into this category fall all dramatic compositions, the finest example of which is Kalidasa's *Abhijnanashakuntalam*.

All other kinds of compositions are broadly classified as shravya.

Shravya kavya may be of three kinds:

- Padyam, or compositions written purely in verse. These are the most common form of shravya kavya; based mainly on their length, they are further divided into two groups:
  - Mahakavya or 'great poem'; this includes Kalidasa's epics, *Raghuvamsham* and *Kumarasambhavam*; and
  - Khandakavya or 'small poem'; this group includes all other lyric poetry in Sanskrit, such as Kalidasa's *Ritusamharam* and *Meghadutam*.
- Gadyam, or compositions written purely in prose. Such compositions are relatively rare in Sanskrit literature; they are often divided by rhetoricians into two groups:
  - Katha, the narration of stories invented by the poet, such as Banabhatta's romance, *Kadambari*; and
  - Akhyayika, the narration of what is known, that is, of legends or tales regarded as true, such as Banabhatta's *Harsha Charita*.
- Mishram, or compositions written in a mixture of verse and prose; these are called champu.

Natya, mahakavya, and khandakavya have been the most popular forms of literary composition in Sanskrit. Kalidasa has left the mark of his genius on all three forms.

Sanskrit poetry does not depend on rhyme or accent but is composed in different metres or arrangements of syllables called chhandas. A poet's skill is often measured by the number of metres he uses in his works. Kalidasa has used a variety of metres, appropriate to mood and theme, in his compositions.

The Order of His Works

We do not know the order in which Kalidasa composed his poems and plays. Scholars give a tentative chronology based on his development as a poet over time – his choice of more and more complex themes, his increasingly nuanced use of language and expression, his deepening understanding of the human condition. Based on such analyses, *Ritusamharam* is regarded by scholars to be his earliest work; it is generally agreed that it was followed by the play *Malavikagnimitram*. These two early works were probably followed by the play *Vikramorvashiyam*, after which came the two epics *Raghuvamsham* and *Kumarasambhavam*, in that order and both incomplete. *Meghadutam* and *Abhijnanashakuntalam* are judged to be his last works.

His Style and Themes

His style is distinguished by his use of literary devices, particularly the simile; yet his language remains light and musical, conveying nuances of mood and feeling with delicacy and grace. Though his themes are varied – from a celebration of the seasons in *Ritusamharam* and court intrigue in *Vikramorvashiyam* to the epic dignity of *Raghuvamsham* – every one of his works is a love poem. Love in union, love in separation, love lost, and love regained – he speaks of all the many aspects of this most complex of human emotions with sensitivity and deep understanding. His affinity with nature is another motif that runs through all his writings. Flowers, plants, birds, and animals – all come to life in his verses.

So accurate, detailed, and vivid are his descriptions of the natural world that we are almost bodily transported to the lush forests, swift-flowing streams, and snowy mountain peaks of his poems and plays. He is no less skilled in his description of the busy cities and royal courts of ancient India and takes us deftly from one world to another, from forest to city, from ascetic ashram to kingly palace. He is equally adept at descriptions of war and military campaigns – his account of Raghu's campaign of world conquest in *Raghuvamsham* is among the finest.

Kalidasa remains the most translated of all Sanskrit poets, in Indian as well as European languages. New translations of his works are continuously undertaken – sometimes in their original metrical form, sometimes in prose – by scholars of Kalidasa and translators distinguished in the field. One or the other of his poems and plays may be read in most of the major Indian languages and many of the European ones. Translations of his works are also available in Persian. His poems are often set to music and performed as dance dramas; his plays, particularly *Abhijnanashakuntalam*, are still performed, on stage as well as the screen. It is a measure of his greatness as a poet that his poems and plays, more than 1,500 years after they were composed, continue to enchant, captivate, and entertain. Anything that can be said about the elegance, power, and beauty of Kalidasa's poetry, or his exalted place in India's literary landscape, is not enough.

Let us now turn our attention to his individual works. In writing this book, I had the privilege of following one of the greatest creative minds the world has seen. In the next three sections of this book, I have attempted to give my readers a glimpse of the wondrous worlds of his lyric poems, plays, and epics. I have summarized each work and explained its setting, structure, impact, and significance. Accompanying the summary of each work are excerpts from an English translation of the work. Different translators bring different styles and approaches to translation, and this is true for Kalidasa's works as well. Some translators follow Kalidasa faithfully, stanza by stanza, line by line, using verse or prose or a mix of the two to reflect the original as closely as possible. Others are not so tightly bound by the form and structure of the original, choosing to highlight its mood and tone instead. The excerpts, which I have chosen from a mix of recent and older translations, reflect some of these varying styles and philosophies. I hope, despite its shortcomings, this book will give my readers – those who are already somewhat familiar with the poet as well as those who are meeting him for the first time – an appreciation of Kalidasa's great works.

Rohini Chowdhury
London, 2025

KHANDAKAVYA
or lyric poetry

'Ritusamharam' and 'Meghadutam'

A lyric is a modern and primarily Western form of poetic composition. It is defined as a poem in which poets express their personal emotions; it is melodious and is closely allied to music. The true lyric is rare in Sanskrit – poetry is highly stylized and composed according to strict rules that determine its form and structure. The individual poet and his personal feelings are not important until transformed into and expressed as artistic sentiment. The closest approach to a lyric poem in Sanskrit is the khandakavya or 'short poem', the poetic classification under which fall Kalidasa's *Ritusamharam* and *Meghadutam*.

Kalidasa's lyric poems represent the start of a new movement in Sanskrit literature, away from epic poetry. Unlike the epics, *Ritusamharam* and *Meghadutam* have no storyline. They are concerned not with battles, wars, and court intrigue, but with the workings of the human heart; their focus is not external, but internal. Shringara or Love, examined in all its subtle nuances, is the main concern of both poems. *Ritusamharam* deals mainly with love in union, when the lover and his beloved are blissfully together; *Meghadutam* is concerned with the anguished longing of separated lovers. Unlike much of modern poetry, Kalidasa's poems celebrate only married love.

It may be argued that passages of great lyrical power – such as the deeply personal hymns by the sage Vasishtha to Varuna in the *Rigveda*, Rama's outpourings of grief at Sita's abduction in the *Ramayana*, and Draupadi's lamentations in the *Mahabharata* – are found in earlier Sanskrit literature. However, the exploration or description of human emotion is not the main focus of these earlier works as it is in Kalidasa's two poems. Every stanza of Kalidasa's two lyrics is complete in itself. Although an integral part of the whole work, it does not need the rest of the poem to give it meaning or context – unlike the long and interdependent passages of epic poetry.

In addition to Love, the second important theme in both *Ritusamharam* and *Meghadutam* is Nature. Kalidasa was a keen observer of the natural world, and his descriptions of even the smallest flower are vivid, detailed, and accurate. The lotus is a recurring motif in his poetry – not just in his lyric poems, but also in his epics and plays. For Kalidasa, the lotus represents purity and grace, and no description of feminine beauty is complete without a comparison with the flower. The lotus also adds to a woman's beauty – as she holds it in her hand or wears it as an ornament on her person. In his eyes, nature adds to the beauty of women, while women, in turn, adorn it.

Love and Nature are Kalidasa's two preoccupations; they are not separate, but entwined, one with the other, each enhancing, affecting, and reflecting the other. We see this in all his works, but especially so in *Ritusamharam* and *Meghadutam*. Love, as Kalidasa depicts it, is not some remote spiritual ideal, but real and very sensuous. His lovers ache for each other when they are apart and are joyous when they are together. They are one with Nature, and Nature, with its changing moods and seasons, its varied landscapes, plants, and animals, is one with them.

Most poems in Sanskrit begin with a benediction or an invocation to a deity. Such a verse is absent in both *Ritusamharam* and *Meghadutam*; the omission gives both poems a secular tone worth noting.

'Ritusamharam' or The Gathering of the Seasons

Ritusamharam is a short poem that describes the seasons through the eyes of a lover. It is generally accepted as one of Kalidasa's early works, perhaps even his first. Though it is considered by many to be far below the literary standard of his later works, it is notable for the poet's sensitivity of expression and his detailed descriptions of the natural world. It stands alone in Sanskrit kavya literature as the only poem to be devoted solely to a description of the seasons.

Structure

The poem's title 'Ritusamharam' is derived from the conjunction of two Sanskrit words: *ritu* or 'season' and *samharah* or 'collecting, gathering or bringing together'; it thus means, quite literally, 'the gathering of the seasons'.

The original text of *Ritusamharam* is in four-line stanzas; in its most generally accepted version, the poem is made up of a total of 144 stanzas arranged into six sections, called sargas or cantos. Some manuscripts contain additional stanzas – these, it is now agreed, are additions made over time to the original text.

The Indian year is divided into six seasons: spring, summer, the rains, autumn, early winter, and winter. The length of each season is two months. In the Indian lunisolar calendar system, the seasons are closely associated with the months. The length of a month is determined by the waxing and waning of the moon, and therefore, so is the duration of a season. In *Ritusamharam*, Kalidasa describes the six seasons in successive cantos; each canto of the poem is devoted to one season and one season alone and is complete in itself. The title gathers the six cantos into a single poem.

Though the Indian year begins with spring, Kalidasa begins his poem with summer and ends it with spring, the season of hope and renewal. In ancient India, spring marked the beginning of the new year. Men and women celebrated its advent with music, dancing, drinking, and general revelry. This festival was known as the Vasantotsava or the Spring Festival. During this time, Kama, the god of love, and his wife, Rati, were also worshipped, together with their friend and helper, Vasanta or Spring. An important part of the festivities was the performance of specially commissioned plays and poems. Kalidasa's play, *Malavikagnimitram*, was presented on the occasion of the Spring Festival. It is very likely that *Ritusamharam* was also composed for and presented at the festival; if so, it is apt that his celebration of the seasons culminates with Spring.

The cantos in order and the number of stanzas in each are as follows:

1. Grishma (summer, the hot season)	28 stanzas
2. Varsha (the rains)	28 stanzas
3. Sharad (autumn)	26 stanzas
4. Hemanta (early winter, the season of frost)	18 stanzas
5. Shishira (winter, the cold season)	16 stanzas
6. Vasanta (spring)	28 stanzas

Kalidasa uses as many as eight different poetic metres across the six cantos.

Ritusamharam is not merely an objective description of the seasons. It is, rather, a love poem, in which the beauty of Nature and feminine beauty are inextricably entwined. Each season is different, distinguished from all others by the way the sunlight falls or the wind blows, the flowers that bloom, the birds that call; each season also brings its own mood and affects the hearts of lovers in its own special way. As the beauty of Nature changes in each season, so does the beauty of Woman – and the emotional response of the lovers (as well as the reader's) to both.

The poet depicts the woman's world – her clothes, jewellery, and flower ornaments, her perfumes and careful make-up of face and eyes and lips – in fine and delicate detail. He is sensitive to her beauty as well as to the inner longings of her heart. His descriptions, though sometimes startlingly intimate, are never prurient. He imagines a young lover who describes to his beloved the changing seasons – their beauty, in his eyes, reflects her own – and the feelings each season arouses in him and every pair of lovers. The poem is a personal statement of the lover to his beloved, its tone that of someone telling a story, rather than writing it. But, like all great works of literature, it is universal in its applicability and true for every lover everywhere. The poem is, moreover, a celebration of young love with all its joys and hopes, still unaffected by the sorrows and disillusionment of age.

Summary

The poem opens with a description of the north Indian summer. In this fiercest of seasons, heat and dust storms stifle the earth and the traveller away from home. Ponds and streams dry up. The fish die, the wild cranes fly away, and thirsty deer in search of water rejoice at the sight of a mirage. The cobra forgets its natural enmity with the peacock and takes refuge from the heat under the shade of its feathers. The lion and the elephants forget to fight, and frogs leap out of the mud of the marsh and sit under the serpent's hood in search of shade. As the heat increases, a mighty forest fire breaks out and devours the dry grass and forest trees, its flames as red as the unfolding petals of palasha flowers. The wild animals flee the forest to take refuge in a low-lying riverbed. In this burning heat, the only relief comes at night, under the silvery beams of the moon. Women dress in fine linen and soft white silk, and wear cooling sandal paste and strings of pearls upon their breasts; in the cool of the night, men enjoy wine and sweet music upon the flower-fragrant terraces of their mansions and turn their thoughts to love.

Then comes the season of rains with its dark clouds, like a king with his war elephants. Lightning flashes, thunder rolls, and life-giving rain floods the thirsty land. The scorched earth regenerates – shoots of jade-green grass appear and new foliage on plants and trees. Insects – red, green, purple, and gold – adorn the earth like jewels. Peacocks call joyously to the rain clouds and spread their gorgeous feathers in a mating dance. The forested slopes of the Vindhya mountains are green again, and full of flowers and herds of grazing deer. Swollen rivers, grey with silt, rush to meet the sea, and wild elephants, in their mating frenzy, challenge the rumbling clouds. Lovers welcome this season with joy, as suppliants their king. Young women, dressed in soft white linen, adorn their hair with flowers. The rain-laden breeze is cool and fragrant with the scent of flowers, and lovers hurry to be together. Young wives, frightened by the lightning and crashing thunder, nestle close to their husbands. The wives whose husbands are away, wait restlessly for their return. The lonely traveller, who has still not returned, remembers the delicate beauty of his wife at home. Though the rainy season brings life and plenty, who in this season, asks the lover, does not sometimes feel a twinge of melancholy?

The rains abate, and autumn arrives, calm and bright; clad in white kasha blossoms, she is as lovely and graceful as a bride. The autumn sky, free of storms, is a translucent blue by day and lit by a silver moon and innumerable stars at night. The harvest of rice stands ripening in the fields, lakes and ponds are white with lotuses and water lilies, the rivers white with waterbirds. The rivers, their waters clear and free of mud, no longer rush, but like beautiful women lost in thoughts of love, wind unhurriedly on their way. The breeze, fragrant with the scent of flowers, carries upon it the tender calls of mating swans and the cries of migratory birds. In this season of smiling abundance, whose heart is not stirred by desire? Women, their hearts bright with love, adorn themselves for their lovers; they dress their dark hair with jasmine flowers and tuck blue lotus buds behind their ears. The day lotus blooms with the rising sun like a lovely

woman's face, but the night lotus fades with the setting of the moon like the smile that slips from the face of a woman whose husband is going away. The clear, cool rays of the moon delight the hearts of lovers but are like poisoned arrows for the young wife separated from her husband.

The lilies and lotuses of autumn fade away, to be replaced by the fresh, young green of barley shoots and the cream-coloured clusters of lodhra blooms. The falling dew now ushers in the season of frost. Though the wind is icy and cold, and the flowers of autumn are faded and pale, young women are happy as they prepare for a night of love with their men. Lovers sleep side by side, entwined in each other's arms. In the morning sunshine, women rejoice at their memories of the night.

The cold increases till it is full winter. The sugarcane stands tall and lush, the paddy is green in the fields, and the fresh, clear air is filled with the calls of cranes and wild geese. Though the winter nights sparkle with stars, they are piercingly cold and cannot be enjoyed outdoors. Young wives retire to their warm rooms and forgive their husbands for their faults. The long nights of the northern winter are sweetened with wine and made warm with passionate love.

At last comes Spring, armed with his arrows of mango blossoms to pierce the hearts of lovers. The trees are in full bloom, the ponds and lakes are covered with lotuses and water lilies, and the breeze is flower-scented. Young women put on colourful garments and wear again the necklaces and jewellery they had removed in winter. In this sweetest of all seasons, love is everywhere – in the mating call of the male cuckoo, in the buzzing of the bees, in the mango trees bursting with flowers, and in the hearts of young lovers. Love makes beautiful women languid with desire; their hearts are full of yearning, and young men are consumed by love for them. In this season of love, the traveller longs for his beloved wife, and weeps to see the mango blossoms.

In the first stanza of every canto, the speaker (the lover) introduces the season he is about to describe to his beloved; in the last stanza, he summarizes the virtues of the season and calls down blessings upon his beloved and the audience. The poem ends with the speaker calling upon Kama, the god of love and conqueror of the world, assisted by his friend Spring, to bring bliss and joy to the audience.

And so the cycle of the seasons continues. Each season is glorious in itself; all six, gathered together in pleasing harmony, make up the year.

Commentaries, Editions, and Translations

Only two old commentaries on *Ritusamharam* have been found so far. The first, called *Chandrika*, was composed by Manirama, son of Nilkantha, in 1814. This is not a very detailed commentary. The other commentary, by one Amarakirti, is known to us only through one manuscript.

Ritusamharam is also the first Sanskrit text of which an edition was printed and published – in 1792 in Calcutta (now Kolkata), by the Asiatic Society of Bengal.

The poem was first translated into English in its entirety in 1942 by Ranjit Sitaram Pandit. A scholar, writer, and successful lawyer, he took an active part in India's struggle for independence and joined Mahatma Gandhi's non-cooperation movement in 1927. He served many terms in prison under the British, and it was over two such prison terms, in 1941 and 1942, that he undertook the translation of Kalidasa's poem. He died in 1944, at the age of fifty-one, his health broken by his long stays in prison. His translation, which he titled *The Pageant of the Seasons*, was published after his death in 1947. Since then, other complete translations of *Ritusamharam* into English have appeared – notably Chandra Rajan's *The Gathering of the Seasons* (1997) and A.N.D. Haksar's *Gathering of Seasons* (2018).

In addition to translations into English, some fifty modern translations of *Ritusamharam* exist in various Indian languages, including Bangla, Gujarati, Hindi, Kannada, Maithili, Malayalam, Marathi, Odia, Punjabi, Telugu, and Urdu.

A Glimpse into 'Ritusamharam'

From Canto 1: SUMMER

The tongues of the flames have the fiery tinge
Of the opening petals of the palasha bloom,
The conflagration like glistening sindura is vermilion;
Swiftly it spreads by the force of the whirlwind,
And embracing the tender leafage
Of creeper and brushwood and tree,
Is filled with a wild ecstasy;
And many a glad and green recess
Is soon burnt to cinder and ashes. 24

From Canto 2: THE RAINS

Green, like fragments of jade,
The grass rises on tiptoe,
Stretching its blades to catch the raindrops;
And a mass of blithe new foliage
Bursts from the kandali plants,
And indragopaka insects make a crimson riot;
With patches of green and purple and gold,
The good earth is decked with many coloured jewels,

Like a woman of elegant taste
And charm of mellowed ease. 5

Touched by the moisture-laden clouds,
The humid breeze is cool
And fragrant with the blossoms
Of kadamba, sarja, arjuna and ketaki
Whom it mirthfully shakes;
Who does not feel, in the quiet of content,
That something's amiss —
An ache in the heart,
Or a tinge of sorrow! 17

From Canto 3: AUTUMN

Her fair visage is the white lotus bloom,
The tinkling of her anklet bells is heard
In the tuneful cry of wild geese on high;
The harvest of rice with ripening sheaves,
Bending in billows in the fresh young breeze,
Is her graceful figure and supple body;
She emulates the charming bride
With white bridal vesture and lily-like face,
The jingling anklets and slender figure,
And the shoulders bowed with decorous modesty
And woman's gentle grace. 1

From Canto 4: EARLY WINTER

The fields covered to the furthest bournes
With rich crops of paddy,
And their fringes adorned with herds of deer,

And the midlands resounding with the distant cry
of the beautiful demoiselle crane
Which stirs the hearts of men. 8

The lakes, where the decorative lily is blooming,
And the amorous kalahamsa blends its grace,
The limpid waters and verdant weeds,
Steal the hearts of men. 9

The priyangu creeper, my love,
Is mellow and pale,
Swept by the wings of the icy wind,
Like the pallid face of the charming maid
Pining for her absent lover. 10

From Canto 5: WINTER

To slam casements and window panes
Of living rooms is a joy,
Welcome are the blazing fires of faggots
And the warmer lazy sunbeams;
One longs now for heavier garments;
'Tis for youthful maidens
The true season for enjoyment. 2

The starlit-nights of winter,
Decked with the sparkling constellations,
Are icy cold with frost,
And colder still by moonlight,
In the piercing chill,
They are not enjoyed in the open air. 4

From Canto 6: SPRING

The languid perfection of the day
Wanes to a quivering twilight,
And all that breathes, or moves, or blossoms,
Is sweeter, my love, in Spring. 2

The male cuckoo, crazy with joy,
Imbibing mango juice,
Is drunk as with wine,
And lovingly kisses its sweetheart;
And even the buzzing bee,
In the folds of the lotus petals,
Murmurs sweet nothingness,
And compliments its mate. 14

The mango trees are a blaze of colour,
The new foliage flecked with coppery sheen,
And their bursting blossoms,
Swinging as they list in the breeze,
Dazzle the minds of maids,
And they catch their breath
With golden new excitement. 15

– from *Ritusamhara* or The Pageant of the Seasons,
translated from the original Sanskrit by R.S. Pandit

'Meghadutam' or The Cloud Messenger

Meghadutam, literally 'cloud-messenger', is Kalidasa's finest poem and one of his most popular works. A masterly and sensitive exploration of love in separation, it ranks among the world's great love poems. It is evident, from its nuanced and layered complexity, that it was composed in the poet's later years, probably towards the end of his poetic career. The poem has no story; it tells us only that a certain yaksha was banished for a year by his master for neglecting his duties. The approach of the rainy season intensifies his longing for the young wife he has had to leave behind. Noticing a rain cloud resting upon the crest of Ramagiri, the Vindhya peak upon which he lives in exile, he decides to send the cloud (*megha*) as a messenger (*duta*) – from which comes the title of the poem – to his wife waiting for him in their home in the city of Alaka on faraway Mount Kailasa. The poem is also called *Meghasandesa* ('the cloud's message') in some manuscripts, or sometimes, simply, *Megha*.

Structure

Meghadutam is a short poem, consisting of 110 to 113 four-line stanzas. In some versions, it is longer, but the extra stanzas are generally regarded as later additions. It is written uniformly in the melodious and majestic Mandakranta metre, which consists of seventeen syllables in each quarter verse. This intricate metre with its long lines is well-suited to the mood of tender melancholy that runs throughout the poem; the metre is also considered, in Sanskrit poetry, appropriate for describing journeys and the rainy season.

In Mallinatha's commentary, the text of the poem is divided into two parts:

- Part 1, called 'Purva Megha', consists of the first 65 stanzas of the poem. Stanzas 1–12 form the introduction to and establish the context and setting of the poem; stanzas 13–65 describe the route the cloud must take from Ramagiri to Alaka.

  The description of the cloud's journey is a cartographic tour de force, displaying Kalidasa's detailed and accurate knowledge of the land. It is also a remarkable poetic achievement. Every place the cloud must pass, every sight it sees or sound it hears is described in evocative detail – rocky mountain slopes and jewelled cities, mangoes glowing golden in the monsoon light, silver fishes jumping in the waves of dark blue rivers, the tinkling of anklet bells, the fragrance of flowers and incense, dancing peacocks, and wild herds of elephant and buffalo, all imbued with the intense and tender longing that only parted lovers know.

The yaksha asks the cloud to detour through Ujjayini, even though the city is not on its way. This is significant, for it shows the special place the city holds in the poet's heart. Kalidasa devotes more lines to Ujjayini than to any other place the cloud must pass, and his descriptions of the city are so intimate and detailed that it has led scholars to suggest it as the city of his birth.

- Part 2, called 'Uttara Megham', consists of the remaining stanzas and describes Alaka, the yaksha's home, and finally, the yaksha's message of love and reassurance to his wife.

The yaksha's longing, which runs like a silver thread through the poem, and the constant presence of the cloud tie the two halves together into a unified poem greater than the sum of its parts.

Summary

Yakshas are semi-divine beings associated with water, forests, and wild places. Their female counterparts are called yakshis or yakshinis. They are the attendants of Kubera, the powerful god of wealth who owns the treasures of the world and lives in the wondrous city of Alaka upon Mount Kailasa. Stories about yakshas and yakshis abound in folklore, mythology, and the epics. Kalidasa's banished yaksha may have been based on a well-known folktale current in his times, one, moreover, that was familiar to his audience – for, beyond the bare facts that 'a certain yaksha' was banished by his lord for failing to perform his duties, Kalidasa tells us no more.

However, it is equally possible that the setting for this poem was entirely a product of the poet's imagination. The yaksha and his wife are never referred to by name; they thus become every pair of parted lovers.

A story, if there was one, has since been lost. Though the old Sanskrit commentaries do give the story of the yaksha's dereliction of duty and consequent exile in brief outline, we cannot be certain that this tale was known to Kalidasa. There are two versions of the story. In the first version, Kubera gives the yaksha the job of looking after his beautiful gardens, particularly the holy Manasa Lake full of golden lotuses. The yaksha, newly married, is constantly distracted by thoughts of his wife and becomes neglectful of his duties. Once, yearning to be with his bride, the yaksha leaves the garden unattended. In his absence, the celestial elephant Airavata gets into the garden and destroys the golden lotuses. In the second version of the story, Kubera entrusts the yaksha with the daily task of gathering fresh lotuses from the lake at dawn for his morning worship of Shiva. The yaksha, reluctant to leave his wife so early in the morning, once gathers the lotus buds in the evening, ready to take up to Kubera the following day at dawn. Unfortunately for the yaksha, a bee has been trapped in the closed lotus buds. The following morning, as the lotuses open and Kubera takes the flowers to offer to Shiva, the bee flies out and stings his finger. Kubera realizes that the yaksha had picked the flowers the previous evening.

In both stories, the yaksha's carelessness ruins Kubera's morning worship. When he realizes that the cause for this neglect was the yaksha's intense desire to be with his wife, he banishes him for a year. The yaksha is forced to leave Alaka and spend the year of his exile separated from his beloved. He also loses all his magical abilities. The yaksha takes up residence in a hermitage upon Ramagiri (literally, 'Rama's hill'), a lofty peak in the Vindhya mountains where, it is believed, Rama spent part of his exile with Sita.

Kalidasa does not narrate the background story but takes us straight to the banished yaksha atop Ramagiri. Deprived of his powers, wasted with the grief of separation from his young wife, he is a sad and lonely figure. Eight long months of his exile have passed, and only four remain. On the first day of the rainy season, he sees a dark cloud clinging to the mountain peak, shaped like an elephant playfully butting the mountain with its head. Overcome with longing, he suppresses his tears with great difficulty. He is worried about his beloved's life, and anxious to find a way to reassure her, to tell her that he still lives and would soon return. As he stands there gazing at the cloud, he is struck by a thought – to send the cloud to his wife with a message. Delighted at the idea, he welcomes the cloud with joy and an offering of fresh kutaja flowers. He is so deep in love that he does not pause to consider whether a cloud, which is only mist, light, wind, and water, could in fact carry messages that only living beings can convey, and entreats it to go to Alaka to his wife.

The yaksha then explains to the cloud the route it must take from Ramagiri to Alaka; this takes up the next 40 stanzas of the poem. The yaksha describes the places the cloud must pass, its resting spots, and the sights it will see on the way. Bidding farewell to Ramagiri, helped along by the breeze and accompanied by wild swans, the cloud must turn north towards Alaka. Along the way, it will cross plateaus and mountains, forests, rivers, towns, and cities. As it approaches, showering the burnt earth with raindrops, trees will burst into bud and blossom, bees, deer, and wild elephants will follow its route, and peacocks will welcome it with joyous cries. It will need to rest from time to time, which it may do upon a lofty mountain peak, or replenish itself when needed by sipping the waters of rivers it passes along the way.

The cloud, after leaving Ramagiri, must ascend the nearby plateau. Then, moving west and then north again, it must fly to the mountain Amrakuta; after quenching the forest fire and resting a while upon its peak, it should then soar across the Vindhya mountains where it would see the River Narmada broken into rivulets by the mountain's rocky sides, its flow impeded by jamun trees. The cloud would then pass over Dasharna country till it reaches its capital, Vidisha, on the banks of the River Vetravati. After sipping the waters of the river, it should rest a little on Nichai hill, where kadamba trees will be in full bloom.

The yaksha then exhorts the cloud to turn towards Ujjayini – even though it is not directly on its path north, it must not miss seeing this magnificent city. It must cross the River Nirvindhya, after which it will reach the country of Avanti, where the tales of Udayana, king of Vatsa, are well known; there, on the banks of the River Shipra, lies the city of Ujjayini. In that bright and glowing city, the cloud would see busy markets full of pearls and jewels for sale, lofty palaces and mansions with flower-filled terraces. It would see the Mahakala temple, set in gardens cooled by the breeze from the River Gandhavati; staying till sunset, it should join in the evening worship with its thunder. The cloud should pass the night with its lightning-wife upon some high roof where pigeons roost, but resume its journey again at dawn.

Next, says the yaksha, the cloud would cross the River Gambhira and reach the temple to Skanda, the war god,

upon Devagiri. After worshipping the god by showering his temple with raindrops and encouraging the god's peacock-steed to dance with its thundering, it must cross the River Charmanvati to Dashapura, a land known for the beauty of its women. It must not miss Kurukshetra, the battlefield where Arjuna showered his arrows upon the heads of kings. After drinking the waters of the Saraswati, it must go to the Ganga, near Kanakhala hill, where she descends from the mountains to the plains. Upon reaching the Himalayas, the cloud is invited to rest a little upon a mountain peak and then make its way to Kailasa upon whose peak stands Alaka, where the yaksha's beloved lives. Thus ends the first part of the poem.

In the second part of the poem, we move from the human world, where the exiled yaksha at present resides, to the magical, mythical world of Alaka, to which he yearns to return. The cloud, impelled by the yaksha's longing for his bride, is our bridge.

In the next few stanzas, the yaksha describes the beautiful city of Alaka, where jewelled palaces touch the sky, flowers bloom all through the year, and peacocks never lose their shining feathers. The nights are always moonlit, the houses bright with lamp-like jewels. There is no sorrow in Alaka – the only tears are those of separated lovers – and youthfulness is the constant condition of its inhabitants, the yakshas. So that the cloud may not miss it, the yaksha then describes his house, which stands, amid flowering trees and with its bejewelled archway, to the north of Kubera's palace. There the cloud will find the yaksha's wife, young and beautiful, but grown thin with grief, her eyes swollen with weeping. The cloud will see her, absorbed in thoughts of her husband, or counting the days that remain before he returns.

The yaksha then instructs the cloud to present itself to his wife, and in its deep voice give her his message. The cloud must reassure her that her husband is alive and tell her of his love and longing for her. It must remind her the curse will end once the season of rains is past, so only four months remain till they are together again, that she must not give in to despair but wait for the bright autumn nights when they will be with each other again. He begs the cloud to return with a message from his wife. The yaksha then hopes that the cloud will consent to be his messenger, and wishes that, having done this favour for him, it may wander where it pleases with its splendour growing ever greater in the rainy season. The poem concludes with the yaksha's fervent prayer that the cloud may never be separated from the lightning, its wife, for even a moment.

At the end of the poem, we find ourselves standing exactly where we were at its beginning, upon Ramagiri's peak, with the lonely yaksha pining for his beloved. Though we have never left the hilltop, we have made the journey from Ramagiri to Alaka, in our hearts and in our minds.

Manuscripts and Commentaries

Meghadutam, like Kalidasa's other works, has come down to us not as the poet composed it, but in several recensions or versions from all parts of India. The poem has been immensely popular since ancient times, a fact indicated by the very large number of original manuscripts that have come down to us – belonging to one recension or the other, in various regional scripts such as Devanagari, Bengali, Nepali, Maithili, Newari, Telugu, and Grantha. The manuscripts are held in libraries in India and abroad. More than a hundred *Meghadutam* manuscripts have been found and catalogued in Nepal; seventeen of these are dated. Among the Nepali manuscripts is also the oldest known manuscript of Kalidasa's poem. This is dated 1363 CE and is written, in the hand of a single scribe, in Newari script on palm leaves; this is also the only known manuscript of *Meghadutam* written on palm leaves. It is held in the National Archives of Nepal in Kathmandu. The two oldest paper manuscripts of *Meghadutam* are dated 1545 CE and 1560 CE.

More than 50 old Sanskrit commentaries on *Meghadutam*, from across the country, are known to us; each of these commentaries also contains a version of the poem. The earliest of the old commentaries is *Panjika*, by the Kashmiri scholar Vallabhadeva, written probably during the early years of the tenth century CE; this pre-dates the oldest available manuscript by some 400 years. *Bala-Prabodhini* by Sthiradeva is another early commentary; though we do not have exact dates, this is most likely later than Vallabhadeva's commentary. Manuscripts of Sthiradeva's commentary have been found across India.

Important commentaries from southern India include *Pradipa* by Dakshinavarta-natha, dated c. thirteenth century CE, and *Vidyullata* by Purna-sarasvati and *Sanjivani* by Mallinatha, both composed during the fourteenth century CE. Commentaries from Bengal include *Tatparya-dipika* by Sanatana Gosvami (c. fifteenth century CE) and the relatively recent, eighteenth-century *Subodha* by Bharata-mallika. Commentaries from western India are mainly by Jain writers, the earliest and best-known of whom is Charitravardhana.

The name of his commentary is unknown, though it is sometimes referred to as *Charitravardhani*. It has been variously dated, from the last years of the fourteenth century to the latter half of the fifteenth century CE.

Most of the important old Sanskrit commentaries are now available in print.

Various versions of the poem had already begun to emerge by the time the oldest of these commentaries was written. Commentators, depending on the text-traditions to which they belonged, took up different versions of the poem, giving them a fixed form which we see reflected in the existing manuscripts (most of which are later than the commentaries). The versions contained in the various commentaries differ considerably from each other in the order as well as the number of stanzas they contain, which varies from 110 stanzas (for example, in the commentaries from Kerala) to as many as 127 stanzas (as in the versions presented by the Jain poets of western India). No two manuscripts of Kalidasa's poem are exactly alike, not even those belonging to the same recension, for, as we had seen earlier, in copying a text, scribes made their own mistakes, corrections, and additions.

Adaptations

Kalidasa's *Meghadutam* has been adapted and used by writers and poets for their own purposes from very early times. One such use was by the Jain monk and scholar Jinasena, who was also the spiritual adviser of the Rashtrakuta king, Amoghavarsha I (reigned 814–878 CE). Soon after the king, his patron, ascended the throne,

Jinasena composed his *Parshvabhyudaya* (The Triumph of Parshva), a biography in verse of Parshvanatha, the twenty-third tirthankara of the Jains – and incorporated into it the complete text of *Meghadutam*. In 1894, Kashinath Bapu Pathak (1850–1932), a professor of Sanskrit at Deccan College in Pune, published an edition of *Meghadutam* based on the text contained in Jinasena's *Parshvabhyudaya*. As Pathak explains in the introduction, in each stanza of his work, Jinasena borrows, in their original sequence, one or two lines from *Meghadutam*; the rest of the stanza is composed by Jinasena himself. In this way, he expertly weaves Kalidasa's entire poem into his work.

The process of proposing part of a stanza to another to be completed is known in Sanskrit as *samasya-puranam* (where *samasya* is the part given to be completed and *puranam* is its completion). According to the rules of this process, explains Pathak, Jinasena had to accept Kalidasa's verses as he found them; he could not change them in any way, for to do so would have been to acknowledge himself an incompetent and inferior poet, and face the ridicule of his peers. Jinasena's incorporation of Kalidasa's poem into his own is seamless; the arrangement of his verses is such that later scribes and commentators cannot easily change or add to them, for amending Jinasena's lines would require a change in the lines from *Meghadutam* – which is precluded by the rules of *samasya-puranam*.

Thus, we can be certain that the text of *Meghadutam* as preserved in *Parshvabhyudaya* is the poem, complete and unchanged, as it was known to Jinasena in the later years of the eighth century CE; this version of the poem consists of 120 stanzas. Jinasena's date is only a century and half later than the two earliest mentions of Kalidasa by name, the Aihole inscription (634 CE) and Banabhatta's *Harshacharita* (c. 600–650 CE); we have discussed both earlier, in our introductory chapter. The version of *Meghadutam* contained in Jinasena's work is the earliest version of the poem known to us (and therefore considered by Pathak to be the most authoritative, a view disputed by scholars such as Eugen Hultzsch).

Kalidasa's poem is similarly used in *Nemiduta*, a devotional poem in honour of Neminatha, the twenty-second Jain tirthankara, by the Jain poet Vikrama, son of Sanganu. The fourth line of every stanza of *Nemiduta* is the same as the last line of one of the stanzas, in order, from *Meghadutam*. Though Vikrama's date is uncertain, he was definitely later than Jinasena.

The poem has also been studied by the Buddhists. The Tibetan *Tengyur* (also known as *Tanjur* or *Bstan-'gyur*, or 'translation of teachings' in Tibetan), a collection of commentaries on the Buddha's teachings and part of the Tibetan Buddhist canon, contains a Tibetan translation of *Meghadutam*, consisting of 117 stanzas; this was translated into German and published in Berlin in 1907. A Sinhalese paraphrase of the poem was discovered in Kandy; it was published in Colombo, Sri Lanka, in 1893, together with the Sanskrit text. The Sinhalese paraphrase contains 118 stanzas.

Meghadutam is often classed as a duta-kavyam or messenger-poem; the first of its kind, it was imitated by many later poets. At least sixteen imitations of the poem are known, of which the earliest is the twelfth-century *Pavanaduta* ('wind-messenger'), by Dhoyika, the court poet of the Sena king Lakshmana Sena of Gauda (present-day Bengal). Messenger-poems inspired by *Meghadutam* are also found in Sinhalese literature; the oldest of these dates back to the fourteenth century CE.

Modern Editions, Translations and Adaptations

The *editio princeps* (i.e., the first printed edition of a work that has hitherto existed only in manuscript form) of *Meghadutam* was published in 1813 in Calcutta by Horace Hayman Wilson, then Secretary of the Asiatic Society of Bengal, together with an English translation and extensive notes. The following year, Wilson's translation was reprinted in London. It was greeted with admiration by Western writers and poets, particularly Goethe. Since then, Kalidasa's poem has been printed and translated innumerable times, in India as well as abroad.

Modern scholars, Western as well as Indian, have tried to reconstitute the poem as it might have been composed by Kalidasa. In doing so, they have attempted to take into account the many different versions of the poem available to us. Given the enormous number of manuscripts, commentaries, and adaptations that exist, this is no easy task. Many editions of the poem, based on different manuscripts and commentaries, have been published since Wilson's edition. The more important of these include the edition by Johannes Gildemeister, published in Bonn in 1841, and that by A.F. Stenzler, published in Breslau in 1874. Stenzler, following Mallinatha's *Sanjivani*, divided the poem into two parts.

In 1894, the same year that Pathak brought out the version of *Meghadutam* as contained in Jinasena's text, G.R. Nandargikar's edition was published in Bombay. In preparing his edition, Nandargikar collated more than 20 manuscripts, which included as many as six commentaries.

This was the first time that such a large number of manuscripts had been used in the preparation of an edition of the poem.

In 1911, Eugen Hultzsch's edition of *Meghadutam* was published, based on the commentary by Vallabhadeva. This was considered definitive by many scholars and is the basis for several modern translations of the poem.

In 1956, a critical edition of *Meghadutam*, prepared by the Sanskrit scholar Sushil Kumar De, was brought out. In preparing his edition, De consulted a number of Bengali, Devanagari, and southern Indian manuscripts. In the introduction to his work, he provides a comprehensive discussion of the old manuscripts, commentaries, translations, and adaptations available, as well as the many modern reconstituted editions of the poem since Wilson's edition of 1813.

Kalidasa's *Meghadutam* remains as popular in India today as it was 1,500 years ago. Several modern commentaries and more than 150 modern translations of the poem exist in English and several Indian languages, including Assamese, Bangla, Gujarati, Hindi, Kannada, Maithili, Malayalam, Marathi, Odia, Punjabi, Tamil, Telugu, and Urdu. The poem is also often set to music and sung or performed as a dance-drama in schools and colleges across the country.

A Glimpse into 'Meghadutam'

The yaksha describes his home in Alaka to the cloud so that it may recognize it and know where to find his beloved.

There, northward from the master's palace, see
Our home, whose rainbow-gateway shines afar;
And near it grows a little coral-tree,
Bending 'neath many a blossom's clustered star,
Loved by my bride as children of adoption are.

A pool is near, to which an emerald stair
Leads down, with blooming lotuses of gold
Whose stalks are polished beryl; resting there,
The wistful swans are glad when they behold
Thine image, and forget the lake they loved of old.

And on the bank, a sapphire-crested hill
Round which the golden plantain-hedges fit;
She loves the spot; and while I marvel still
At thee, my friend, as flashing lightnings flit
About thine edge, with restless rapture I remember it.

The ashoka-tree, with sweetly dancing lines,
The favourite bakul-tree, are near the bower
Of amaranth-engirdled jasmine-vines;
Like me, they wait to feel the winning power
Of her persuasion, ere they blossom into flower.

A golden pole is set between the pair,
With crystal perch above its emerald bands
As green as young bamboo; at sunset there
Thy friend, the blue-necked peacock, rises, stands,
And dances when she claps her bracelet-tinkling hands.

These are the signs—recall them o'er and o'er.
My clever friend—by which the house is known.
And the Conch and Lotus painted by the door:
Alas! when I am far, the charm is gone—
The lotus' loveliness is lost with set of sun.

Small as the elephant cub thou must become
For easy entrance; rest where gems enhance
The glory of the hill beside my home,
And peep into the house with lightning-glance.
But make its brightness dim as fireflies' twinkling dance.

From the yaksha's message of love and longing, which he asks the cloud to deliver to his wife:

I see thy limbs in graceful-creeping vines,
Thy glances in the eyes of gentle deer,
Thine eyebrows in the ripple's dancing lines,
Thy locks in plumes, thy face in moonlight clear—
Ah, jealous! But the whole sweet image is not here.

And when I paint that loving jealousy
With chalk upon the rock, and my caress
As at thy feet I lie, I cannot see
Through tears that to mine eyes unbidden press—
So stern a fate denies a painted happiness.

And when I toss mine arms to clasp thee tight,
Mine own though but in visions of a dream—
They who behold the oft-repeated sight,
The kind divinities of wood and stream,
Let fall great pearly tears that on the blossoms gleam.

Himalaya's breeze blows gently from the north,
Unsheathing twigs upon the deodar
And sweet with sap that it entices forth—
I embrace it lovingly; it came so far,
Perhaps it touched thee first, my life's unchanging star!

Oh, might the long, long night seem short to me!
Oh, might the day his hourly tortures hide!
Such longings for the things that cannot be,
Consume my helpless heart, sweet-glancing bride,
In burning agonies of absence from thy side.

Yet much reflection, dearest, makes me strong,
Strong with an inner strength; nor shouldst thou feel
Despair at what has come to us of wrong;
Who has unending woe or lasting weal?
Our fates move up and down upon a circling wheel.

When Vishnu rises from his serpent bed
The curse is ended; close thine eyelids tight

And wait till only four months more are sped;
Then we shall taste each long-desired delight
Through nights that the full autumn moon illumines bright.

– from *Kalidasa: Translations of Shakuntala and Other Works* by Arthur W. Ryder

NATYA
or drama

'Malavikagnimitram', 'Vikramorvashiyam' and 'Abhijnanashakuntalam'

Drama in ancient India reached its zenith during the early centuries of the Common Era, with the plays of the ancient Sanskrit dramatists. Foremost among these works are Kalidasa's *Abhijnanashakuntalam*, Sudaraka's *Mricchakatikam* (Little Clay Cart; fifth century CE), and Bhasa's *Swapnavasavadattam* (The Dream of Vasavadatta; first or second century CE). Other important plays include *Mudrarakshasa* (The Minister's Ring; c. sixth century CE), a political intrigue set in the time of Chandragupta Maurya, by Vishakhadatta; *Uttararamacharita* (Rama's Last Act; eighth century CE), derived from the *Ramayana*, by Bhavabhuti; and *Ratnavali* (seventh century CE), a romantic court drama by Harsha. The earliest of the great Sanskrit dramas were written during the first or second century CE, and the last during the eighth or ninth century CE. This period, spanning almost a thousand years, is regarded as the golden age of drama in India.

Most of what we know about the theory and practice of ancient drama is drawn from the *Natyashastra* (Treatise on Drama), the oldest and most comprehensive text on drama and dramatics available to us. Attributed to the sage Bharata, it was probably put together by several authors sometime during the second century CE. As the celebrated Sanskrit scholar V. Raghavan explains in his essay 'Sanskrit Drama: Theory and Performance' (published in 1967 in the journal *Comparative Drama*), the *Natyashastra* ascribes an origin as ancient as the Vedas to the dramatic arts. It tells us that natya is made up of elements extracted from the four Vedas: the spoken or recited word from the *Rigveda*, song from the *Samaveda*, action from the *Yajurveda*, and sentiment from the *Atharvaveda*. In Sanskrit, *natya* means and consists of both dance and drama, and drama, as envisioned in the *Natyashastra*, is the combined art of poetry, music, and dance.

Kalidasa, universally acknowledged as the greatest of the Sanskrit dramatists, brings together all three forms with unparalleled skill and finesse. In addition to his masterpiece, *Abhijnanashakuntalam*, two more of his plays, *Malavikagnimitram* and *Vikramorvashiyam*, survive to the present day. He sums up the essence of the ancient drama in a passage in *Malavikagnimitram*:

> Natya is a charming spectacle to be enjoyed by the eye, as pleasing to the gods as a sacrifice. Shiva, the Cosmic Dancer, blends in this art his fierce dance of creation with the gentle dance of Uma, his consort. The deeds of men, the result of qualities both good and bad and giving rise to varied moods and emotions, are depicted in natya. The art of drama is the delight of all humankind, though their tastes be different.*

Kalidasa follows the rules laid down by Bharata only in broad outline. It is more likely that he preceded the

*Translation by the author, based on other translations and commentaries

Natyashastra, and that the *Natyashastra* is based on Kalidasa's dramas rather than the other way around.

The Elements of a Sanskrit Drama

The three essential constituents of every Sanskrit drama are vastu or plot, nayaka or hero, and rasa or sentiment.

The plot or subject matter of the play may be entirely made up or drawn from history, myth, or epic; it may also be a combination of these. For instance, consider Kalidasa's three plays – *Malavikagnimitram* is based on historical events, *Vikramorvashiyam* on a story found in the Rigveda, and *Abhijnanashakuntalam* on the story of Shakuntala in the *Mahabharata*. According to the *Natyashastra*, one of the important aims of Sanskrit drama is to create a harmonious experience for the spectators, so all plays were required to have happy endings. Sanskrit dramatists would change even well-known stories to achieve this objective. Kalidasa, too, modifies the stories of Urvashi and Shakuntala to give his plays a pleasing conclusion.

Heroes can be of four kinds: dhirodatta or one who is brave and noble-minded; dhiroddhata, who is brave but haughty; dhiraprashanta, who is brave and calm; and dhiralalita, who is brave and firm, but light-hearted and reckless. Kalidasa's heroes – Agnimitra in *Malavikagnimitram*, Dushyanta in *Abhijnanashakuntalam*, and Pururava in *Vikramorvashiyam* – are all dhirodatta heroes. The nayaka's female counterpart, the nayika, who may be his wife or another woman he is in love with, must have similar qualities.

The *Natyashastra* also describes other important character types. One such is the vidushaka or court jester, who is usually a childhood friend and constant companion of the hero. Endowed with wit and wisdom, he helps the hero sort his romantic tangles. The vidushaka Gautama in *Malavikagnimitram* is the perfect example of this character type. The nayika, too, has close female friends or companions. They have qualities similar to those of the hero's friends; devoted and loyal to the nayika, they often play the role of confidante and help her through her romantic trials. Shakuntala's friends Priyamvada and Anasuya in *Abhijnanashakuntalam* exemplify this character type. Other kinds of characters described in the *Natyashastra* include the leader of the king's army, members of the king's court, junior queens, concubines, courtesans, ascetics, priests, merchants, traders, and male and female slaves and attendants – we meet many of these character types in Kalidasa's plays.

According to the *Natyashastra*, the most important constituent of drama is rasa or sentiment. This is the primary mood or 'flavour' of the drama, the lasting and all-absorbing feeling it evokes in the hearts of the audience. It is produced by the action and interaction of all the other elements, major or minor, that make up play. Poetry, music, song, and dance, the portrayal of diverse emotions such as love or laughter, compassion or anger called for in the story and experienced by the characters, the costumes, jewellery, and make-up of the actors, the setting of the play, the season in which the main action might take place, even the layout and structure of the theatre in which a play is performed – all work together towards the creation of rasa. Plot and character are also subservient to rasa. Without rasa, there is no natya.

The primary rasa in all three of Kalidasa's plays is Shringara or Love. In his plays, as in his poetry, Kalidasa's main concern is romantic love in all its forms and its impact on the human heart. For Malavika, as for Shakuntala, love is a new experience, intense and all-consuming. For Malavika, its consummation brings a place in the royal harem as the king's favourite wife; for Shakuntala, it brings years of heartbreak, loneliness, and single parenthood before she can occupy her rightful place at Dushyanta's side. Urvashi, as an apsara, is experienced in the ways of men, but her love for Pururava is no less intense; she gives up her place in the celestial realms for him and, bound by the laws of heaven, willingly suffers separation from their son to be with him.

For the men, too, love brings both joy and sorrow. Agnimitra is restless to possess Malavika and knows no peace till he can marry her. Dushyanta, cursed to forget his beloved Shakuntala, is tortured by memories he cannot access, while Pururava, who is willing to give up his entire world for Urvashi, is driven to the edge of madness by her sudden disappearance. And that is not all.

Others, too, are affected by the love between hero and heroine. For instance, the chief queens and other wives of the kings replaced by their new loves have to deal with their husbands' wandering hearts. They must come to terms with rejection and heartbreak and, setting aside pride and jealousy, accept their rival with as much dignity as they can muster.

Throughout every play, the moods and feelings of the characters are reflected in the natural world. In *Abhijnanashakuntalam*, Shakuntala's world is the forest, and she, kin to trees and animals, almost a nature-spirit herself. In *Vikramorvashiyam*, the king's grief and despair at being separated from Urvashi is sharpened by the beauty of the forests and groves through which he wanders. Even in the light-hearted *Malavikagnimitram*, the king sees the beauty of his beloved reflected in the beauty of the golden Ashoka tree and yearns for her even more.

The ancient Sanskrit dramatists wrote their plays to be performed rather than to be read or studied, for it is only through performance that rasa is fully achieved. The ancient dramas were performed by professional theatre troupes patronized by royal courts and wealthy merchants. Plays were usually staged on special occasions, such as coronations and festivals. For instance, we know from its prologue that Kalidasa's play *Malavikagnimitram* was written for and performed for the celebration of the Vasantotsava or Spring Festival.

Staging a Sanskrit Drama

In addition to advice on how to write a play, the *Natyashastra* lays down detailed guidelines for its production and performance, including instructions for the building of the natyamandapam or theatre, even specifying the type of bricks to be used and the acoustical effects to be achieved. Private theatres in palaces and the homes of wealthy merchants were decorated with sculptures and ornamental woodwork; these were meant for small, select audiences. Plays were also performed in temple squares or open-air theatres for larger, more general audiences. Certain types of plays were considered appropriate for the morning, others for the afternoon or the evening. Performances could last for a few hours, a full day, or even longer.

Every dramatic performance began with a prologue. This included an opening benediction, after which the sutradhara or stage manager would, with the help of an assistant or sthapaka, introduce the poet and the play. All of Kalidasa's three plays begin with an invocation to Shiva. Plays were usually divided into ankas or acts, four to ten in number. Kalidasa's *Malavikagnimitram* and *Vikramorvashiyam* are each five acts long; *Abhijnanashakuntalam* consists of seven acts. An act was made up of scenes, though scene divisions were not indicated. The end of an act was marked by the exit of all the characters. The play ended with the Bharatavakya (so called in honour of the sage Bharata) or epilogue, consisting of the last few lines or verses of the play.

There was little or no scenery or props. Locations, scenes, settings, even the time at which the action was taking place were described by characters and singers on stage or off. Parts of the stage were shown, through word or action, to represent certain locations, such as gardens or the banks of a river. So a character may go from one location to another without leaving the stage or any pause in the performance. Stage directions were sparse. Stylized movements, borrowed from dance, were used to depict actions such as driving a chariot, rowing a boat, dismounting from a horse, or even throwing a stone.

Women were not excluded from performance and often played the female roles. Costumes, jewellery, and make-up were important, and conveyed important information about the characters to the audience. For instance, in Act 3 of *Vikramorvashiyam*, the queen, Aushinari, engaged in the performance of a vow, enters appropriately attired in white, with strands of sacred durva grass woven into her hair and wearing only a few jewels to indicate her married status. On the other hand, Urvashi, the apsara with whom the king has fallen deeply in love and who returns his passion, enters dressed and veiled in deep blue like a woman going secretly to meet her lover under cover of the night. The contrasting costumes instantly convey the tension in the scene as well as the opposing roles of the two characters.

Since the objective of natya was to create a pleasing experience for the spectator, certain events and actions were never depicted on stage. These included events that were boring or too long, such as journeys; trivial actions, such as eating or drinking; and actions considered improper or too intimate, such as kissing. Since it was more important to depict the effect of an event rather than the depiction of the event itself, unpleasant or sensational events like the death of the hero, or war, fire, or massacres were not shown on stage. They could, however, be described by a character.

Sanskrit plays were written in a mixture of prose and verse in various poetic metres. A mixture of languages was also used: the hero and other important male characters used Sanskrit, the language of the learned; women (except courtesans, who spoke in Sanskrit) and less-educated male characters spoke in various Prakrit dialects. The words were usually recited or sung, though they may also have been spoken. They were also enacted visually through dance or hand gestures, mime, and facial expressions borrowed from dance. Emotions, events, and actions could also be enacted visually through dance – as in Act 4 of *Vikramorvashiyam*, which depicts through song and dance the grief-induced madness of Pururava as he searches for his lost love, Urvashi. Such visual enactments helped those in the audience who had difficulty following Sanskrit or the different types of Prakrit used in the play. Ancient temple sculptures as well as extant classical dance forms such as Bharatanatyam, Kathakali, and Kuchipudi give us a glimpse of dance as used in ancient dramatic performances.

Music, vocal and instrumental, was used throughout the performance. Vocal music, in the form of songs known as dhruvas, was the more important. The dhruvas were composed in specific metres, in both Sanskrit and Prakrit. They were accompanied by the veena, the flute, and drums such as the mridanga or the pushkara, and, upon completion, would often be illustrated or explained through dance. They were usually sung offstage, but could also be sung onstage, sometimes by the leading characters themselves, to emphasize a particular emotion, signal a change of mood, mark the entry or exit of a character, or indicate the end of an act. Songs and music were also used to fill gaps in action on stage – for instance, if a character fell unconscious. In most cases, the songs were not written by the dramatist as part of the play but composed by the singers and musicians involved in its performance. The original music and melodies, passed down orally from one generation of musicians to the next, have been lost over time.

By the tenth century CE, Sanskrit drama was in decline. New plays were written to be read, not performed, and lost the vitality of the ancient plays. The tradition died out, and of the hundreds of plays that must once have existed, only some 40 of the great dramas survive today.

'Malavikagnimitram' or Malavika and Agnimitra

Malavikagnimitram is Kalidasa's earliest play. It is also his shortest, consisting of a total of 95 stanzas in five acts. It is considered by many to be far less accomplished in terms of technical and poetic skill than his later plays and lacks their intense, emotional impact. Nevertheless, it is an elegant and skilfully constructed drama, light-hearted and clever, with none of the pathos that characterizes his other plays. It is essentially a drama about love, and tells the story of Agnimitra, ruler of Vidisha, and his love for the beautiful Malavika, an attendant of his chief queen, Dharini. As the king's friends scheme to bring Agnimitra and Malavika together, the queen plots to keep them apart; this leads to complicated situations that make the audience laugh out loud.

The romance, located in the small and private world of the inner apartments of the palace, is set against the larger world of politics, war, and battles; the events in the two worlds intertwine to culminate in an ending as satisfying to the characters as to the audience. Though *Malavikagnimitram* is not as celebrated in modern times as Kalidasa's other plays, it is a finely crafted and charming example of Sanskrit drama and a tribute to Kalidasa's versatility.

Setting

Unlike Kalidasa's other two plays, which are drawn from myth and epic, *Malavikagnimitram* is set in historical times, in the second century BCE, during the reign of Emperor Pushyamitra, the founder of the Shunga dynasty. The scene is laid in Vidisha, the second capital of the Shunga empire, where Agnimitra, Pushyamitra's son and heir, rules as his viceroy. The romance between Agnimitra and Malavika has no basis in fact. However, the setting Kalidasa has given his play is more or less historically correct, and the characters of the emperor, Pushyamitra Shunga, his son and successor, Agnimitra (the hero of Kalidasa's play), and Agnimitra's son and heir, Vasumitra, in the play are people who existed in history. (Neither Pushyamitra nor Vasumitra appears on stage, but both are mentioned in the play.)

Coins, inscriptions, and contemporary records give us some idea of the actual events of this period. Pushyamitra Shunga was the senapati or commander-in-chief of the ninth Mauryan emperor Brihadratha. In 185 BCE, he assassinated Brihadratha during a military parade and usurped the throne of Magadha (part of present-day Bihar). This brought about the end of the Mauryan dynasty and the establishment of

Shunga rule in northern and central India. Pushyamitra is referred to in Kalidasa's play as 'Senapati', an indication that he may have retained his title of commander-in-chief even after he became emperor.

Pushyamitra extended his empire north-west as far as Sialkot in present-day Pakistan, and to west-central India to the Malwa plateau, to the cities of Ujjayini and Vidisha. He ruled his expanding empire from Pataliputra (modern Patna), the old capital city of the Mauryas. As the Shunga territories expanded, the city of Vidisha became the empire's second capital, from which Agnimitra governed the faraway southern provinces on his father's behalf. The River Narmada marked the southern borders of their empire.

During the expansion and consolidation of his territories, Pushyamitra Shunga came into conflict with the kingdom of Vidarbha on the southern border of the Shunga Empire in what is east-central Maharashtra today. He also led many campaigns against the Yavanas or Bactrian Greeks in the north-west, thwarting their attempts to expand into the Gangetic plain. Kalidasa alludes to many of these events in his play.

Pushyamitra is known to have performed several ashvamedhas or horse-sacrifices to legitimize his rule. The ashvamedha was an elaborate and important sacrifice performed by a king to display his power. First, the sacrificial horse would be sent forth to roam at will for a year; it was followed by armed warriors who would claim, on behalf of the king, any territory through which the horse passed and battle all those who opposed its passage. At the end of the year, the horse would be brought back and sacrificed with great ceremony. In the final act of his play, Kalidasa refers to an ashvamedha performed by Pushyamitra – he gives the responsibility of guarding the horse to his grandson, Agnimitra's son Vasumitra, who successfully brings the horse back after defeating a contingent of Yavanas.

While a few historians point to Buddhist texts such as the *Divyavadana* mentioning that Pushyamitra persecuted the Buddhists, it is not a definitive claim. In Kalidasa's play, the Shungas are presented as tolerant and liberal rulers, particularly Pushyamitra's son and viceroy, Agnimitra, who is ever respectful and considerate towards Kaushiki, a Buddhist ascetic in the queen's retinue.

Pushyamitra Shunga ruled for approximately 36 years, till 149 BCE, when he was succeeded by Agnimitra, who was already ruling as viceroy in Vidisha. Agnimitra ruled till 141 BCE when he was succeeded by Vasujyestha, probably his brother; Vasujyestha was followed by Agnimitra's son, Vasumitra. Little is known of the remaining Shunga kings. The dynasty came to an end in 73 BCE when the last Shunga emperor was assassinated by his minister, Vasudev Kanva.

The political action in the play is often underplayed by critics since it is never depicted on stage, and we learn of it only through letters received by the king and brief conversations between him and his ministers or between other, less important, characters. However, it gives the play an edge that makes it far more exciting than a mere palace intrigue. Agnimitra is not just the traditional romantic hero yearning for his beloved; he is also a clever strategist and polished diplomat who wields the reins of kingship with a sure and steady hand. He is sharply aware of the duties of a king, which include fulfilling his roles of son, husband, and father appropriately. Though he has differences with his father, the emperor, his loyalty is unquestioned, and, despite his philandering ways, he is considerate and respectful towards his queen, Dharini, and appropriately proud of their son, Vasumitra.

Agnimitra is the most interesting and well-rounded of Kalidasa's heroes. Neither Pururava in *Vikramorvashiyam* nor Dushyanta in *Abhijnanashakuntalam*, though each a great king in his own right, is shown in any role other than that of a lover. Agnimitra is far more multidimensional, and therefore much more real, than either of them.

The historical setting of the play and the favour shown to Agnimitra has led scholars to suggest that Kalidasa lived during Shunga rule and was the court poet of Agnimitra.

Structure

The play is divided into five acts.

The prologue, at the beginning of the first act, gives us a glimpse of Kalidasa as an upcoming young poet. It starts with an invocation to Shiva – this is true for all of Kalidasa's plays, a fact that is put forward in support of the assertion that Kalidasa was a follower of Shiva. The sutradhara or stage manager then introduces the play and the poet. He begins by explaining that he has been asked to stage a play on the occasion of the Spring Festival, and for that purpose, he has chosen a play by Kalidasa. His assistant objects, saying that it does not seem right to disregard the works of 'older' playwrights such as Bhasa, Saumillak, and Kaviputra in favour of a work by Kalidasa, a 'modern' poet. This statement, in addition to being Kalidasa's way of acknowledging the great playwrights who came before him, also indicates his new and perhaps yet to be established status. Interestingly, while 13 plays of Bhasa, dated to the first or second century CE, have been discovered, nothing is known about the other two poets beyond their names.

The play concludes with the traditional Bharatavakya or epilogue: spoken by Agnimitra at the end of Act 5, it is a prayer for the well-being of his subjects so long as he, Agnimitra, remains their king. As we saw earlier, the Bharatavakya of a Sanskrit play consists of the last few lines or verses of the play. It is in the nature of a benediction, which may be a prayer for the peace and prosperity of the country, a hope for fame and riches for the poet, or wishes for the long life of the ruling king. It is not usual practice to name the king in the epilogue, but Kalidasa specifically mentions King Agnimitra. (The only other Sanskrit play in which the name of the king is mentioned in the epilogue is *Mudrarakshasa* by Vishakhadatta.) Since the king mentioned in the Bharatavakya is usually the king in whose reign the play was composed and first performed, the epilogue to this play is often quoted to support the theory that Kalidasa was Agnimitra's court poet.

Kalidasa uses 21 different metres across the 95 stanzas of the play.

Characters

The hero or nayaka of the play is the brave and noble king Agnimitra, ruler of Vidisha. The heroine or nayika is Malavika, a beautiful young woman in the retinue of Dharini, his chief queen. Dharini is a woman of some importance in the royal household – she holds the title of Queen Consort and is the mother of Agnimitra's son and heir, Vasumitra. After the king, his vidushaka or jester, Gautama, is the most important character in the play. He is the king's childhood companion and closest friend. Utterly loyal, quick-thinking, and clever, he schemes to bring Agnimitra and Malavika together.

Other important characters include Iravati, Agnimitra's junior queen and his favourite until he falls in love with Malavika, and Kaushiki, a female ascetic in the retinue of Queen Dharini. Among the less important characters are Bakulavalika, the queen's principal attendant, and the rival dance instructors Ganadasa and Haradatta. Vahatava, the king's chief minister, and Maudgalya, the chamberlain in charge of the royal household, and various guards and attendants are some other – minor – characters.

Several characters are mentioned in the play but do not appear on stage. These include the Shunga emperor, Pushyamitra (he is also known as 'Pushpamitra', which is the name used by Kalidasa); Vasumitra, Agnimitra and Dharini's son; Virasena, Dharini's half-brother and the commander of Agnimitra's forces; Yajnasena, ruler of Vidarbha; Madhavasena, Yajnasena's rival and cousin; and Sumati, the chief minister of Vidarbha. Bards and musicians also sing and play from behind the curtain.

Summary

The actions depicted on stage take place over a period of three weeks, in the royal palace and its surroundings pleasure groves and gardens. The season is spring.

At the start of the play we are introduced to the palace attendants Bakulavalika and Kaumudika, both of whom serve Queen Dharini. We learn from their conversation that the queen has appointed the dance instructor Ganadasa to tutor her attendant Malavika and has sent Bakulavalika to inquire about her progress. Kaumudika is on her way back from the jeweller, from whom she has collected the queen's signet ring with a serpent seal. This ring becomes important later in the play.

We also hear that the king, Agnimitra, has seen by chance a picture of Malavika in a group portrait of Queen Dharini and her retinue. He is so struck by Malavika's beauty that he can think of little else; the queen, aware of her husband's infatuation, is taking every care to ensure that the young woman is kept as far away from him as possible. We then meet Ganadasa, who praises Malavika's extraordinary talent for music and dance, and asks Bakulavalika about her, who explains that Malavika was sent to the queen as an attendant by her half-brother Virasena.

Virasena is also Agnimitra's commander-in-chief, and by the king's orders, is in command of the border fortress on the River Narmada, along the southern frontier of the Shunga empire. This is an important assignment, for south of the Narmada lies Vidarbha, an erstwhile vassal state of the Mauryas, which is now intent on breaking away from the overlordship of the Shungas.

We now meet Agnimitra and Chief Minister Vahatava, who is holding a letter from Yajnasena, king of Vidarbha. The letter gives us the political setting of the play. We learn that Yajnasena has married the sister of the Mauryan minister, thus making clear his rejection of Shunga rule. In retaliation, Agnimitra has taken his brother-in-law prisoner. We also learn that Yajnasena's cousin Prince Madhavasena has set himself up as his rival and laid claim to the throne of Vidarbha. Unsuccessful against Yajnasena, he has entered into negotiations with Agnimitra for an alliance through marriage. He and his wife have set off for Vidisha with his sister, whose hand he has offered in marriage – we do not know, as yet, to whom, for Yajnasena's letter gives us no hint whether Madhavasena intends his sister to marry Agnimitra, or his son and heir, Vasumitra.

However, Madhavasena is intercepted at the border by one of Yajnasena's commanders and taken prisoner. Agnimitra demands the immediate release of Madhavasena and his wife and sister. Yajnasena's letter – that we see in Vahatava's hand – is in response to this demand. It is a dignified and reasonable letter, which requests that Agnimitra remain neutral in the affairs of Vidarbha. He explains that Madhavasena's sister was lost in the confusion at the border, but that he would make every effort to find her. He then proposes an exchange of prisoners, offering to release Madhavasena if Agnimitra releases his brother-in-law. This infuriates Agnimitra and he immediately orders an expedition against Yajnasena under the command of Virasena.

The affairs of state taken care of, at least for the moment, Agnimitra turns his attention to the equally pressing matter of his desire to see Malavika in person. He tasks his friend and companion, the vidushaka Gautama, to make this wish come true. The rest of Act 1 and most of the rest of the play is taken up by Gautama's various schemes to fulfil the king's desire. He contrives to cause a quarrel between the dance instructors Ganadasa and Haradatta as to who is the better teacher. Ganadasa is favoured by Queen Dharini, who has also put him in charge of tutoring Malavika; Haradatta, his rival, is favoured by the king.

A contest is proposed, in which each instructor proposes to show off his best student. The king decrees that the issue must be decided in front of Queen Dharini, lest he be accused of partiality. He also requests the presence of Kaushiki, a female ascetic in the queen's retinue. Dharini, who realizes that the contest will put Malavika directly in front of the king, is reluctant, but ultimately agrees. This ends Act 1.

Act 2 is devoted to the contest, which takes place the following day. Ganadasa's student, Malavika, is asked to perform first. This gives the king the opportunity he has been seeking – he gazes at her loveliness to his heart's content as she sings and dances. Malavika, unaware of the king's passion for her, is also secretly in love with him. She cannot express her feelings directly but takes the opportunity to do so through her singing and dancing. Since the objective of the contest has been achieved, the performance of Haradatta's student is postponed. The Act ends with the king declaring to Gautama that Malavika, now that he has seen her, rules his heart to the exclusion of all the other women in his harem.

At the beginning of the next Act, we learn that Ganadasa has been declared the winner of the contest, that the king is quite madly in love with Malavika, and that Queen Dharini is taking even more care to keep her away from him. Meanwhile, Gautama tells the king that he has managed to enlist Bakulavalika, the queen's principal attendant, for their cause. He also reminds the king of his promise to his junior queen, Iravati, to meet her in the pleasure grove attached to the royal palace. When Agnimitra objects, Gautama reminds him that as the king he must continue to be courteous to his queens, regardless of the state of his heart.

They proceed to the pleasure grove, and as they stand there admiring the trees and flowers, Malavika enters. She has been sent by Queen Dharini to perform the rite of dohada for the golden Ashoka tree that stands in the grove. This rite is often mentioned in Sanskrit literature and is derived from the belief that plants, like pregnant women, have intense longings at budding time. The Ashoka, in particular, longs for the touch of a beautiful woman's foot – this causes the tree to burst into bloom. The rite would have normally been performed by Dharini herself, but Gautama has somehow managed to ensure that she falls off a swing and hurts her feet. Dharini has therefore deputed Malavika to perform the rite and has promised her that if the Ashoka flowers within five nights of receiving the touch of her foot, she will grant any wish of hers, whatever it may be.

Malavika waits by the Ashoka tree for Bakulavalika to come with the ornaments the queen wants her to wear for the dohada rite. Gautama draws Agnimitra's attention to Malavika's presence, and the king is overjoyed to see her there and watches, hidden, from a distance.

Malavika, quite unaware of the king, chastises her heart and orders it to stop yearning for the king's love. Bakulavalika arrives with the queen's own anklets, which Dharini desires Malavika to wear. As she begins to adorn Malavika's feet, Iravati enters, accompanied by her attendant Nipunika. She is taken aback to see Malavika being prepared to perform the dohada rite. The king and Iravati are unaware of each other and unseen by both Malavika and Bakulavalika. They overhear their conversation, during which Malavika confesses her love for the king, and Bakulavalika, in accordance with the promise she had made to Gautama, speaks to her about the king's passion for her. At this point, Agnimitra reveals himself, but so does a furious Iravati, whose worst suspicions have been confirmed. Malavika and Bakulavalika, shaken by her wrath, make a hurried exit. Iravati refuses to be pacified by the king and walks off with her attendant.

Act 3 ends with Agnimitra declaring that since Iravati has left in a temper, he can now stop worrying about her with an easy conscience.

In Act 4, we see the consequences of the king's encounter with Malavika in the pleasure grove. Agnimitra enters, accompanied by Jayasena, a female guard of the queen's apartments. He is looking for the vidushaka Gautama, whom he had sent to get news of Malavika. Gautama enters with the news that Iravati had visited Queen Dharini to ask about her injury and had told her what had happened. As a result, Dharini had ordered that Malavika and Bakulavalika be thrown into the underground prison. She had also given strict instructions to their guard Madhavika that the two young women were not to be released under any circumstances unless her own signet ring was produced by the messenger.

The king sighs in despair, but as always, Gautama has a plan, which he whispers to the king. The king, delighted, tells him to go ahead with it. Gautama leaves after a hurried whisper in Jayasena's ear. The king is then led by Jayasena to a veranda where Dharini is resting her injured foot. She is being waited upon by her attendants and the female ascetic, Kaushiki.

Suddenly, Gautama rushes in, shouting in panic, pretending that he has been bitten by a snake while picking flowers for the queen. He is carried away to see the physician Dhruvasiddhi, a specialist in the treatment of snakebite. Jayasena comes in, ostensibly with a message from the physician, asking for an object with the figure of a snake on it to accomplish the cure. Dharini, suspecting nothing, immediately gives Jayasena her signet ring with the serpent seal, the same one that was seen with Kaumudika at the start of the play.

Jayasena leaves with the ring; she returns to say that Gautama has been cured of the snake's venom. Dharini sighs

in relief. Jayasena also gives the king a message, supposedly from his minister, Vahatava, that he is needed immediately to attend to some urgent matters of state. The king uses this message to excuse himself from Dharini's presence. He orders that the queen be moved to a shadier spot, and the queen and her retinue leave.

The king meets Gautama in the pleasure grove, and the vidushaka gleefully recounts the success of his plan. He had shown the queen's signet ring – which Jayasena had promptly delivered to him – to Madhavika, the woman guarding Malavika in her underground prison. He had successfully allayed all of Madhavika's suspicions, who had released Malavika and Bakulavalika. Gautama had then escorted them to a lakeside pavilion.

Agnimitra hurries with Gautama to the pavilion where Malavika is waiting. Bakulavalika and Gautama leave the lovers alone; they mount guard outside the pavilion, Gautama at the door, Bakulavalika concealed in the bushes nearby. Unfortunately, Gautama falls asleep at his post. He is seen by a passing maid, and the news immediately reaches Iravati. She goes to the pavilion with her trusted attendant Nipunika, hoping to find the king there with Gautama. Instead, she finds him with Malavika, and soon uncovers the whole story of Gautama's pretend snakebite and his ruse to get the queen's ring to free Malavika from her prison. Iravati is unforgiving and scathing in her condemnation of Gautama's trick. Agnimitra and Gautama squirm uncomfortably in front of her. The king can see no way out of this situation.

Just then, Jayasena rushes in with the news that the young princess Vasulakshmi has been frightened by a monkey and can't be calmed. Iravati, distracted, urges the king to hurry to the child. The king rushes out, followed by a relieved

Gautama – who thanks the monkey for its timely help! Iravati and her attendants also leave.

Malavika is left behind with Bakulavalika, trembling at the thought of what Queen Dharini might do when she hears of her assignation with the king. Just then, we hear the voice of the keeper of the royal gardens calling out that the golden Ashoka is covered with buds though five nights have not passed since the dohada rite, and that he is on his way to inform the queen of this at once. Malavika and Bakulavalika are overjoyed to hear this; they exit, intending to follow the keeper to see the queen. This brings Act 4 to a close.

In Act 5, the last and final act of the play, we return to the larger world of politics, war, and battles that we had briefly heard about in Act 1. As the Act begins, we hear that the rites to honour the golden Ashoka tree have been completed. We also realize that the emperor Pushyamitra intends to perform an ashvamedha, and that he has given his grandson, Dharini's son, Crown Prince Vasumitra, the dangerous and difficult task of guarding the sacrificial horse. News has also arrived that King Yajnasena of Vidarbha has been defeated by King Agnimitra's forces under Virasena, and that Yajnasena's cousin, Prince Madhavasena, has been released and has sent a caravan of rich gifts to Vidisha as tribute. Several attendants, mainly women accomplished in the arts, have also come with the gifts.

Meanwhile, Queen Dharini has sent a message to her husband – the king – to join her in the pleasure grove so that she may enjoy the glory of the blossoming Ashoka with him. Agnimitra sets off for the grove with Gautama. The king is sorrowful in his yearning for Malavika but happy, too, in Virasena's victory over Vidarbha. He reaches the grove to find Dharini waiting for him with Malavika by her side, which surprises and delights him. Just then, Maudgalya, the chamberlain of the royal household, enters, and announces that two of the women who had arrived with the tribute from Vidarbha and could not earlier be presented to the king, were now ready to be brought before him.

The two girls recognize Malavika as soon as they see her, and prostrate themselves before her, addressing her as 'the princess'. It turns out that she is none other than Prince Madhavasena's lost sister, who had been taken to safety by the prince's prime minister Sumati when the prince had been attacked by Yajnasena on his way to Vidisha.

The ascetic, Kaushiki, now takes up the tale. She confesses that she is Sumati's younger sister, and that when her brother had realized that Prince Madhavasena faced capture by Yajnasena, he had escaped with Malavika and Kaushiki. The three of them had joined a caravan of merchants headed for Vidisha, hoping to reach the king. But the caravan had been attacked by bandits. In the fighting that had ensued, Sumati had been killed, and Kaushiki and the princess separated.

Kaushiki had decided to continue her journey to Vidisha, disguising herself in the saffron robes of a Buddhist ascetic. She had managed to become part of the queen's retinue, and, upon entering the palace, had met Malavika again. The princess had fortunately been rescued by Virasena, who had sent her to his sister, the queen. Kaushiki explains that she had remained silent about Malavika's true identity because of a prophecy that Malavika would have to spend a year in servitude before she could find a husband worthy of her. But with the year now over, Kaushiki could narrate the whole story.

As Kaushiki finishes her tale, Maudgalya returns, this time with a message from Agnimitra's prime minister, Vahatava, asking for the king's opinion on the Vidarbha problem. The king gives his decision: both Yajnasena and Madhavasena are to rule, but independently and separately, one to the north, the other to the south of the River Varada, which was to be the boundary between their two kingdoms. Maudgalya takes the king's message to the prime minister and council of ministers, who have independently reached the same solution. Vidarbha is thus neutralized and no longer a threat to the Shungas.

Maudgalya returns with a letter and a gift for Agnimitra from the emperor. The letter describes how the sacred horse for the ashvamedha, while wandering along the banks of the River Sindhu, had been captured by the Yavanas. A fierce battle had ensued in which the Shunga troops under Vasumitra had been victorious. Since Vasumitra had brought back the sacred horse, the emperor was ready to begin the sacrifice, and desired his son Agnimitra and his daughter-in-law Dharini to attend and participate in the rituals.

Agnimitra and Dharini are overcome with pride and joy at their son's victory. In celebration, Agnimitra orders all prisoners to be freed at once, in particular the brother-in-law of Yajnasena. Dharini, as a token of her happiness, gives Malavika in marriage to the king as was originally intended by the princess's brother, Madhavasena. Since Malavika is now known to be of noble descent, it is fitting that she marry the king and be given the title of 'queen'. The play ends on a note of mutual goodwill and happiness all around.

Inspiration for the Story of Malavika

Kalidasa has set the play against a historical backdrop, but the story is imaginary, with no basis in fact. This is true for the main incidents – for instance, the argument between the dance instructors, Malavika's dance performance, Gautama's various schemes and stratagems, the rite of dohada performed by Malavika for the Ashoka tree, and so on. Interestingly, though, the story of Malavika, in outline, is remarkably similar to the story of Bandhumati from an ancient collection of stories known as the *Brihatkatha* or *Great Tale*, probably compiled sometime during the fourth century CE during Gupta rule. This collection of tales is now lost. Fortunately, several retellings of its stories survive, of which the eleventh-century *Kathasaritsagara* by Somadeva is the longest and most important. Stories about Udayana, the legendary king of the ancient kingdom of Vatsa, and his queen Vasavadatta make up a large portion of Somadeva's retelling. Tucked into one of these tales, we find the following passage:

> The king of Vatsa married a princess called Bandhumati. Gopalaka had taken the princess captive in war; he had then sent her as a present to his sister, Udayana's queen Vasavadatta. The princess was as beautiful as the goddess Lakshmi. So the queen had kept her away from the king, concealing her identity and changing her name to Manjulika. But the king had seen her by chance while with his friend Vasantaka. He had instantly fallen in love and married her secretly in a summerhouse. This event was seen by the queen, who, furious, had Vasantaka put in chains.

The king had then appealed for help to Sankrityanani, a female ascetic in the queen's retinue who had come with her from her father's court. She had appeased the queen's anger and persuaded her to present Bandhumati to the king.*

The parallels between the story of Bandhumati and that of Malavika are obvious. Stories about King Udayana were popular in Avanti and Ujjayini in Kalidasa's times – as the poet himself tells us in his lyric poem, *Meghadutam*. They were also a part of the *Brihatkatha* and served as inspiration for many of the ancient Sanskrit dramatists, including Banabhatta, Harsha, and Vishakhadatta. The story of Bandhumati is mentioned almost in passing in the *Kathasaritsagara*. But Somadeva's text is dated several hundred years after Kalidasa, and it is quite possible that the tale was better known in Kalidasa's times.

Adaptations and Translations

In addition to English, *Malavikagnimitram* has been translated several times into major Indian languages, including Bengali, Gujarati, Hindi, Kannada, Maithili, Malayalam, Marathi, Odia, Punjabi, Tamil, and Telugu. Notable English translations in recent times include Chandra Rajan's *Malavika and Agnimitra* (2002). The play was also made into a silent film, *Malvikagnimitra*, in 1929 by the celebrated film-maker Dadasaheb Phalke.

*Adapted from *The Katha Sarit Sagara*, as translated by C.H. Tawney

A Glimpse into 'Malavikagnimitram'

From Act 3

Malavika, upon the orders of Queen Dharini, has just completed the rite of dohada, striking the Ashoka tree with her foot. The king and his vidushaka, Gautama, concealed behind a creeper, overhear Malavika confess her love for the king to Dharini's attendant, Bakulavalika. The king's junior queen, Iravati, suspects the king is in love with Malavika. Iravati and her attendant, Nipunika, unknown to both the king and Malavika, are also concealed in the garden.

KING.

Oh Ashoka! If after having been honoured by the slender-waisted one with this foot of hers, soft as a young lotus, loud-tinkling with noisy anklets, you are not immediately endowed with flowers, in vain do you nurse a desire shared by sportive lovers.

Friend, I wish to present myself, taking a favourable opportunity of joining in the conversation.

VIDUSHAKA.
Come along! I will tease her.
(*Both enter)*

NIPUNIKA (*to Iravati*).
Queen! Here is the King appearing on the scene.

IRAVATI.
This is exactly what my heart anticipated at the outset.

VIDUSHAKA (*advancing*).
My lady, it is not at all proper conduct on your part to strike with your left foot an Ashoka-tree which is the dear friend of the King.

BAKULAVALIKA AND MALAVIKA *(in a state of trepidation*).
Ah! Here is the King.

VIDUSHAKA.
Bakulavalika! Why did not you as you knew the state of the case, restrain the lady from committing such an impropriety? (*Malavika shows fear.)*

NIPUNIKA.
Queen, see what the noble Gautama has undertaken.

IRAVATI.
How else could a low Brahman like him make a livelihood?

BAKULAVALIKA.
Sir! this lady is executing an order of the Queen's. In this transgression she is only the instrument of another. Let the

King be appeased. (*She makes Malavika prostrate herself, and falls prostrate at the same time.*)

KING.
If this is the case, you are not guilty. My good girl, rise up. (*He takes Malavika by the hand and raises her up.*)

VIDUSHAKA.
Quite right. In this matter you ought to show respect for the Queen.

KING.
Oh! charming one, I hope you do not now feel any pain in your left foot soft as a young shoot, which you placed on hard trunk of the tree? What say you, beautiful girl?
(*Malavika looks ashamed.*)

IRAVATI (*spitefully*).
Ah! My husband has a heart as soft as fresh butter.

MALAVIKA.
Come Bakulavalika, let us inform the Queen that we have performed her command.

BAKULAVALIKA.
Then ask the King to give you leave to depart.

KING.
My good girl, you may go. But hear first my supplication, which now has an opportunity of making itself known.

BAKULAVALIKA.
Listen attentively! Let the King be pleased to speak!

KING.
This person for a long time has not been able to put forth such a blossom of happiness; with the nectar of your touch satisfy also the longing of this man devoted to you alone.

IRAVATI (*suddenly approaching*).
Satisfy it, satisfy it; no doubt the Ashoka shows flowers, but this tree does not only display flowers, it bears fruit also.

(*All are confused on beholding Iravati.*)

KING (*aside*).
My friend, what resource is there now?

VIDUSHAKA.
What other than taking to our heels?

IRAVATI.
Bakulavalika! you have begun well. Malavika! grant the request of my husband.

BOTH THE GIRLS.
Let the Queen have compassion on us! Who are we that we should attract the affection of the King?

[*Exeunt Bakulavalika and Malavika*]

IRAVATI.
Oh the faithlessness of men! I indeed relying upon your deceitful speech – unsuspicious like the deer that is attracted by the whistle of the hunter – did not anticipate this.

VIDUSHAKA (*aside*).
Make some defence at once. Being a thief caught in the hole he has dug through a wall, you ought to say that you came here as a student of the art of digging through walls!

KING.
Beautiful one! I had no object with Malavika. Because you delayed, I amused myself as well I could.

IRAVATI.
You are to be depended on, are you not? I did not know that my husband had obtained such an agreeable means of passing the time. Otherwise, unhappy that I am, I would never have caused this interruption.

VIDUSHAKA.
Do not repel by your speeches the courtesy of the King. If mere conversation with the attendants of our royal mistress when met by chance is to be considered a crime — why, of course, you know best, and we must acquiesce.

IRAVATI.
Well, conversation let it be called. How long am I to torture myself about nothing? (*She goes off in a passion.*)

KING (*following her*).
Forgive me.

(*Iravati keeps walking though her feet are entangled in her girdle.*)

KING.
Beautiful one, neglect of your devoted admirer is not becoming.

IRAVATI.
Traitor, your heart is not to be relied on.

KING.
With the word 'traitor', oh dear one, let your scorn of me, who am so familiar to you, come to an end; you do not dismiss your anger even though entreated by your girdle lying prostrate at your feet.

IRAVATI.
Even this cursed girdle sides with you. (*She takes up the girdle and endeavours to strike the King with it.*)

KING.
This lady in a passion, raining tears, prepares to strike me, terrible criminal that I am, with the cord of her golden girdle fallen unexpectedly from her bimba-like hips, as a row of thunder-clouds to strike the Vindhya mountain with a streak of lightning.

IRAVATI.
Why do you drive me into transgression again (*raising her hand with the girdle in it*).

KING.
Why do you withdraw the scourge lifted against me the malefactor, oh curly-haired one! You increase your

fascinations, and still you are angry with your slave here. (*To himself*) Surely at this time I am permitted to prostrate myself (*falls at her feet*).

IRAVATI.
These indeed are not the feet of Malavika, that will gratify your longing for a caress. (*She departs with her attendant.*)

VIDUSHAKA.
Come! rise up, rise up, you have found favour.

KING (*rising up and not seeing Iravati*).
What? Is the dear one really gone?

VIDUSHAKA.
I am glad to say she has gone without forgiving this impropriety. Therefore let us flee rapidly before she returns like Mars retrogressing to his mansion in the zodiac!

KING.
Oh the inconsistency of love! Now that my mind is taken captive by my beloved, I consider Iravati's rejection of my humble supplication a veritable service; for, as she is angry, I may neglect her, though she is so attached to me.

[*Both walk round and exeunt*]

Here ends the Third Act.

– adapted from *The Malavikagnimitra: A Sanskrit Play by Kalidasa*, as translated by C.H. Tawney

'Vikramorvashiyam' or Urvashi, Won by Valour

Vikramorvashiyam is the second of Kalidasa's three plays. Like his other plays, it is a love story, relating in five acts the mythic tale of King Pururava and the apsara Urvashi. Its plot, drawn from sources as ancient as the *Rigveda*, is straightforward, and the ultimate union of the lovers comes about far more easily than in Kalidasa's first play, *Malavikagnimitram*. Despite the relative simplicity of its plot, it is far more sophisticated than the earlier play in terms of both poetic skill and its exploration of love.

Malavikagnimitram is a cheerful play, and the lovers, though yearning for each other, are never so overcome by love as to lose sight of the rest of the world. In *Vikramorvashiyam*, Kalidasa explores love that is so intense that it becomes all-consuming. Despite the mandatory happy ending required of ancient Sanskrit drama, *Vikramorvashiyam* is a dark play: Pururava's passion for Urvashi is such that it drives him to the point of insanity, and Urvashi's love for him jealous and possessive, so that even in their happiest moments, the lovers are burdened by tragedy. The fourth act of the play – for most of which the only character on stage is Pururava, driven mad by Urvashi's sudden disappearance – is a powerful exploration of the nature of obsessive love.

This play, far more than *Malavikagnimitram*, is also distinguished by Kalidasa's vivacious descriptions of people and events, his invocation of Nature and natural beauty, and his deft use of simile and metaphor. *Vikramorvashiyam* is a far more complex play than *Malavikagnimitram* in the themes it explores and the manner in which they are handled. Though this play does not quite reach the flawless perfection of *Abhijnanashakuntalam*, Kalidasa's third play and final work, it is one of the finest of the ancient Sanskrit dramas.

Title

It is often assumed that the title of the play refers to the king and his beloved, the hero and heroine of the play, and that 'Vikrama' is another name for Pururava. This interpretation is seen in the titles of translations such as Chandra Rajan's *Vikrama and Urvashi* (2002). It has also been suggested that the title of the play, and the several occurrences of the word *vikrama* within it, was a reference by Kalidasa to his patron, whom tradition maintains was a king with the name or title of Vikramaditya.

The literal meaning of *vikrama* is 'courage, prowess, valour', a quality possessed by Pururava, which is referred to several times in the play and which he displays in his rescue of Urvashi. The celebrated scholar H.D. Velankar suggested that the word *vikrama* is used in its literal sense in the title. In the introduction to his translation of the play, he explains the title as meaning 'A drama pertaining to Urvashi, won and retained by valour.' This meaning is reflected in David Gitomer's translation of the play 'Urvashi Won by Valor' (*The Plays of Kalidasa*, UNESCO's Theater of Memory Project, 1984). A.N.D. Haksar touches upon these various interpretations of the title in the introduction to his own translation of the play, *Quest for Urvashi* (2021). He additionally points out that *vikrama* also means 'valour in a quest', which is the meaning reflected in the title of his translation.

Setting

The story of the play is based on the mythological tale of King Pururava, of divine descent and a scion of the lunar dynasty, and Urvashi a celestial dancer in Indra's court. Much of the action on stage takes place in the world of mortals – in the royal palace and the king's pleasure gardens in the city of Pratishthana, located at the confluence of the rivers Ganga and Yamuna. However, the world of gods and demigods is never far away. The opening scenes of the play are set in the skies, along the paths where only celestial beings and those who consort with the gods may pass, and on Hemakuta, a golden peak in the Himalayas. Act 4, the central act of the play, is set initially in some heavenly region in the sky and then in the mythical Gandhamadana forest upon the slopes of Mount Kailasa.

Structure

The play is divided into five acts.

The prologue at the beginning of the first act begins with an invocation to Shiva. The sutradhara or stage manager introduces the play as a completely new drama never staged before and composed by Kalidasa. Given that he does not feel it necessary to give more details about the poet indicates that Kalidasa is now recognized and well-established. The play ends with the customary Bharatavakya.

Act 4 is the distinguishing act of the play. For most of its duration there is only one character on stage – the king, Pururava, crazed by Urvashi's sudden disappearance. His state of mind is depicted almost exclusively through music, song, and dance. Most of the act is a soliloquy by the king; there is no dialogue in this act, except briefly at its beginning and its end. This makes the act unique in Sanskrit drama.

The act is further distinguished by its extensive use of Prakrit dialects. An extraordinarily large number of Prakrit verses, sung by the king on stage as well as by singers offstage, are interspersed with the Sanskrit. These passages were initially questioned by modern scholarship as being later additions and not composed by Kalidasa at all but are now generally accepted as part of the text. They are quite beautiful in themselves, and supplement and complement the Sanskrit.

The play is known for the purity and elegance of its poetry; this also reaches its peak in the fourth act.

Act 4 stands alone, complete in itself, the rest of the play merely a frame for its exploration of the nature of love and its impact. It is often regarded and staged as a musical dance-drama in its own right, independent of the rest of the play.

Not including the Prakrit stanzas in Act 4, Kalidasa uses nineteen metres across the five acts of the play.

Characters

The hero or nayaka of the play is Pururava, the son of Budha (Mercury) and Ila, and the grandson of the Moon. Though divinely descended, he is mortal. He is a powerful king, a skilled warrior, brave and chivalrous. He enjoys the friendship of Indra, king of the gods, who regards him as his ally and comrade-in-arms against the danavas, a race of demons who are sworn enemies of the gods. He is also called 'Rajarshi', or 'royal sage'.

While we are aware of Pururava's great and noble qualities, we see him chiefly in the role of a lover, so deeply in love with Urvashi that he cares nothing for glory or power. He hands over the reins of government without hesitation to his ministers for an unspecified period, just so he can be with his beloved in the Gandhamadana forest. At the end of the play, he is ready to hand his crown and throne to his young son, Ayush, and retire to the forest as an ascetic when it seems that Urvashi must leave him.

The heroine or nayika is the apsara Urvashi, a dancer at Indra's court. Apsaras are celestial women who live in the sky and are usually represented as hauntingly beautiful. They are endowed with magical powers and can change their shape at will. They are also associated with water and are the female counterparts of the gandharvas, celestial musicians who live in Indra's heaven. They are drawn to warriors and heroes.

Apsaras are Indra's chief weapon against sages engaged in rigorous penance – whenever he is afraid that a sage might acquire great power through austerities, he sends down an apsara to distract him, and she usually succeeds. Urvashi is the most beautiful of all the apsaras in Indra's court. She is also the daughter of the ancient sage Narayana (later identified with Vishnu) and therefore has a status higher than that of the other apsaras.

Other important characters are Aushinari, Pururava's chief queen and daughter of the king of Kashi; the vidushaka Manavaka, the king's close friend and companion; and Ayush, the king's son by Urvashi. Aushinari is a somewhat tragic figure – despite being Pururava's principal queen, she has no choice but to accept her husband's love for another woman and ultimately does so in as dignified a manner as the situation allows. Manavaka, though he is the king's confidant, does not play a critical role in the play, except as the accidental agent through whom the queen learns of her husband's secret love for Urvashi. But he is an interesting character – witty, practical, and down to earth. He is a loyal friend and ally who, though understanding of the king's situation, tries his best to restore a sense of normalcy in the face of the king's obsession with Urvashi. In his opinion, a good and timely meal is more important than the sighs of the lovelorn king.

Minor characters include Urvashi's close friend, the apsara Chitralekha; Satyavati, a female ascetic with whom Urvashi leaves her infant son; the divine sage Narada, Indra's messenger; Chitraratha, king of the gandharvas; Latavya, the chamberlain of the royal household; disciples of the sage Bharata; various other apsaras; and attendants of the king and queen.

Key characters who are mentioned but do not appear on stage include Indra, king of the gods; the danava monarch

Keshi, ruler of the golden city of Hiranyapuri; and Bharata Muni, author of the *Natyashastra*.

Bards and musicians sing and play from behind the curtain.

Summary

The action depicted on stage in Act 1 takes place in the skies and on the golden peak of Hemakuta in the Himalayas. The season is spring.

At the end of the prologue, the sutradhara draws the audience's attention to the cries of distress that can be heard backstage. As he exits, a group of apsaras rush onto the stage, calling desperately for help. We learn that Urvashi, together with her friend Chitralekha, has been kidnapped by the danava king, Keshi. Pururava, mounted on his chariot with his charioteer, and on his way back to Earth after paying his respects to the Sun God, answers their cries for help; learning of the abduction, he sets off in pursuit of the danava king. The apsaras descend from the sky and wait anxiously on Hemakuta's peak for his return.

The king returns with Urvashi and Chitralekha, flying through the sky on his chariot. Urvashi, who had fainted with fear, recovers, and Chitralekha assures her that she is safe, rescued by Pururava, equal to Indra in might of arms. The king is captivated by Urvashi's beauty and she by his noble bearing – though at this point neither knows how the other feels. Pururava's chariot descends on Hemakuta's summit and is greeted by the waiting apsaras with great relief.

As the apsaras fuss over Urvashi, the sound of another chariot is heard. It is Chitraratha, king of the gandharvas. Indra, hearing that Urvashi had been kidnapped, had sent the entire gandharva army to rescue her. While on their way, they had heard that Pururava had already defeated Keshi and rescued Urvashi; Chitraratha has therefore come to find him. He explains that he must now take Urvashi back to Indra and invites Pururava to accompany them. Pururava modestly declines, and Chitraratha escorts the apsaras away.

Urvashi falls behind the rest, pretending that her string of pearls has become entangled in a creeper. Chitralekha, understanding her intention, pretends to disentangle the necklace, while Urvashi uses the delay to look back at the king, her eyes full of love. The king returns her glance with equal fervour. As the king prepares to leave, Urvashi casts a last, passionate look at him and leaves with Chitralekha. Pururava gazes yearningly after her, certain that he will never win her love. He exits with his charioteer. This concludes Act 1.

Act 2 is located in the terraces and gardens of the king's palace in Pratishthana. A few days have passed since the events of Act 1. The king is immersed in thoughts of Urvashi. Aushinari, his queen, notices her husband's preoccupation. She commands her attendant, Nipunika, to find out from the vidushaka Manavaka what is troubling the king. As the king's closest friend, Manavaka is privy to the king's secret, but has been commanded by him to tell no one. Nipunika finds Manavaka on his own in a secluded spot by the palace. She engages him in conversation and cleverly tricks him into revealing the king's passion for Urvashi. As Nipunika leaves, an announcement is heard that the royal court has risen for the midday break and the king is on his way. Manavaka hurries to meet the king.

The scene now moves to the royal pleasure gardens. The king, weary with longing, unburdens himself to Manavaka. Meanwhile, Urvashi, driven by her own longing for the king, comes in search of him. She is accompanied by her friend Chitralekha. The two apsaras fly down from the celestial pathway in the sky to the king's gardens. They see Pururava deep in conversation with Manavaka. Urvashi, uncertain of the king's feelings for her, decides to eavesdrop, and the two apsaras make themselves invisible. Using her magical powers, she creates a piece of birch bark, upon which she writes a poem expressing her love for the king. She throws the letter upon the ground in front of the king. Manavaka notices the sudden appearance of the piece of bark and guesses that it might be a message from Urvashi. The king eagerly picks it up and is delighted to find that it is indeed a letter from her. He hands the birch-bark letter to Manavaka for safekeeping.

Urvashi, finally convinced that the king's response indicates that he truly loves her, now decides to show herself. Pururava is overcome. But just then the voice of a messenger from Indra's heaven is heard offstage. The messenger announces that the king of the gods wishes to see performed that very day the play taught to Urvashi by the sage Bharata, and that Urvashi must return at once to perform her assigned part. Indra's command cannot be ignored, so Pururava, though deeply disappointed, gives her leave to go. Urvashi leaves with great reluctance, accompanied by Chitralekha.

Manavaka tries to comfort the king with Urvashi's birch-bark letter but realizes to his dismay that he has lost it. The king curses the vidushaka's carelessness and orders him to find it. As Manavaka searches desperately for the letter, Queen Aushinari enters with Nipunika, who has told her about Pururava's passion for Urvashi. The queen, hearing that the king was in the pleasure gardens with Manavaka, has come there to confirm the truth for herself. Neither the king nor the vidushaka, distressed by the loss of Urvashi's letter, notices the queen, who conceals herself behind some creepers.

Meanwhile, Urvashi's letter is blown by the wind towards the queen. Nipunika picks it up and reads it to her, confirming her suspicions. Aushinari realizes that the king and Manavaka are searching for this very letter. Furious, she steps out from her hiding place and offers the letter to the king. The embarrassed king tries to pacify the queen and falls at her feet, admitting his guilt. But she rejects his show of remorse and stalks out – though she doubts her own resolve to remain angry for very long. The king, while acknowledging that the queen had every right to be furious, declares that his heart now belongs to Urvashi. The two exit, Manavaka eager for his somewhat delayed midday meal, the king pining for Urvashi.

Act 3 begins at the hermitage of the sage Bharata, where two of his disciples are discussing the play staged in Indra's court. From their conversation it seems the sage has just returned to his hermitage after the performance. So the time is probably the evening of the same day as the events of Act 2. We learn from the disciples that the play was *Lakshmi Svayamvara* (Lakshmi Chooses a Bridegroom) composed by the goddess Sarasvati, and that Urvashi played the leading role of the goddess Lakshmi. Unfortunately, Urvashi was distracted and made a mistake. When asked, in the play, whom she had set her heart on, she should have answered 'Purushottam' (a name for Vishnu, Lakshmi's beloved); instead, she answered 'Pururava'. This angered the sage, who pronounced a curse upon her, depriving her of her celestial status in Indra's heaven. But Indra, who looks upon Pururava as his friend and ally, was sympathetic, and softened the sage's curse, saying that she may go to Pururava and live with him till he sees the face of the child that she will bear him.

The rest of Act 3 takes place on the terrace of the Jewelled Palace, one of the king's royal palaces in Pratishthana. The action begins at sunset. A few days have probably passed since Queen Aushinari's confrontation with the king. She is now full of regret for her rudeness and wants to make up for it. She sends word to the king through the royal chamberlain Latavya, inviting her husband to join her on the roof of the Jewelled Palace, where she wishes to worship the Moon till it is united with the star Rohini (the Moon-god's favourite wife). The king, realizing that the queen wants to make amends, accepts her invitation and makes his way to the Jewelled Palace, accompanied by Manavaka. The Moon rises in all its beauty, and while they wait for the queen to arrive, Pururava cannot but dwell on his passion for Urvashi.

Meanwhile, Urvashi and Chitralekha appear, descending from the sky down to earth. Urvashi is dressed like a woman on her way to meet her lover and has come in search of Pururava. They see him on the terrace of the Jewelled Palace and, going closer, overhear his outpourings to Manavaka. The apsaras are both invisible, but before Urvashi can reveal herself to the king, the queen arrives with her attendants. She is dressed simply, as is appropriate for a woman engaged in the observance of a vow. The king greets her with courtesy and affection. The queen performs the ceremony of worshipping the Moon; at the end, she gives her consent to the king's union with Urvashi. The king protests that he is true to her, but the queen, her vow now complete, leaves without more ado. Her attendants follow her out.

Urvashi and Chitralekha, who have witnessed the entire scene, now reveal themselves to the king and Manavaka.

The lovers are happily reunited, this time without impediment, since the queen has given her permission. Chitralekha informs the king that since spring is ending, she must return to her summer duties of attending upon the Sun. She requests the king to look after Urvashi and returns to Indra's heaven. Manavaka urges the king to retire with Urvashi; the king and Urvashi do so, and all leave the stage. Thus ends Act 3.

Act 4 takes place several years after the events of Act 3. It is now the start of the rainy season. The act begins in some part of the heavens, where we see Chitralekha and another apsara called Sahajanya in conversation. We learn that a terrible misfortune has befallen Urvashi and Pururava. The lovers had gone to the sweet-smelling Gandhamadana groves to spend some time together, away from the cares of the court. There, they had seen a young Vidyadhara woman playing along the banks of the Ganga. (Vidyadharas are semi-divine beings who live in the regions between the earth and the sky, and possess magical powers.) The king had gazed at her a little too ardently, which had caused Urvashi to fly into a jealous rage. She had run away from the king, and, blind with anger, had rushed into the grove sacred to the god Kumara (also known as Kartikeya). Her mind was also muddled by the sage's curse, so that she forgot that the grove was forbidden to women. As a result, she was instantly transformed into a creeper at the edge of the grove. We hear that the king, driven mad by Urvashi's sudden disappearance, is still searching for her night and day in the forest. The only means to bring the lovers back together, says Chitralekha, is through the Sangamaniya, the magical jewel of reunion.

The scene now moves to the Gandhamadana forest. The king enters, crazed with grief. He rambles through the forest, talking to himself, pausing to ask the trees and flowers, the birds and animals, even the rain clouds in the sky, whether they have seen his beloved. In the course of his mad wanderings, he accidentally finds the Sangamaniya gem. He picks it up, and with it in his hand, turns towards a slender vine that reminds him of Urvashi. He closes his eyes and embraces it as though it is his lover – immediately, the vine turns into Urvashi, who has been freed from the spell by the touch of the magic jewel. Pururava opens his eyes in disbelief to find that it is indeed Urvashi he is holding in his arms. She explains to him the curse of the sacred grove, and the king, reunited with his beloved, regains his sanity. The lovers return to Pratishthana, riding upon a rain cloud which Urvashi turns into a flying chariot with her magical powers. This blissful event brings Act 4 to a close.

Act 5 takes place soon after Pururava and Urvashi's return from the Gandhamadana forest. The action is situated in the royal palace in Pratishthana. The king is welcomed back with joy by his subjects and courtiers and picks up the reins of government again. He lacks for nothing, except an heir.

Soon after the king's return, a terrible calamity occurs: the bright red Sangamaniya, being taken to Urvashi to wear, is mistaken by a vulture for a piece of meat. The bird swoops down, snatches up the jewel in its beak and flies away with it. Manavaka, hearing of the disaster, hurries to the king, who, already aware of the theft, has called for his bow and arrow. But before his bow-bearer returns with his bow, the vulture has flown away out of his arrow's range. Pururava gives orders for the vulture to be hunted down and the gem recovered.

Manavaka urges the king to relax, reassuring him that the vulture will not escape. The king sits down with the vidushaka, explaining the jewel was important to him not for its value but because it had reunited him with his beloved Urvashi. Just then, Latavya, the chamberlain, enters with the astonishing news that the vulture has been shot by an unknown archer and the gem has been retrieved. The king orders the gem to be washed and purified and returned to its casket. No one knows who has shot the bird, though Latavya says there is a name engraved upon the arrow, but in letters too fine for his weak eyes to read.

The king asks for the arrow and reads what's written on it with mounting surprise and joy. Latavya leaves, and the king remains lost in thought. When Manavaka questions him, the king reads out the inscription on the arrow. It states that the owner of the arrow is Prince Ayush, the son of Pururava and Urvashi. Manavaka congratulates him, but the king is puzzled – except on one occasion, when he had performed a sacrifice in the Nimisha forest, he had never been separated from Urvashi. So when was this son born? He had not noticed any signs in Urvashi that she may be pregnant either, except a certain weariness for a few days. Manavaka reminds him that Urvashi is an apsara, and their ways are different from those of mortal women. Pururava accepts the explanation, but is still puzzled – why did Urvashi hide the birth of their son from him?

Just then, Latavya announces the arrival of a female ascetic and a young boy from the hermitage of the sage Chyavana. Manavaka wonders whether this might be the same boy whose name was inscribed on the arrow. Latavya ushers in the ascetic, who is called Satyavati, and the boy, and Pururava knows at once that the boy is his son. Satyavati confirms it, asking the boy to bow down before his father, the king. She explains that Urvashi had placed the boy in her care the moment he was born, and that he had been brought up in the hermitage as a king's son under the sage's supervision. However, that morning, he had killed a vulture perched on a treetop with a piece of meat in its beak. Such an act was forbidden in the hermitage, so the sage had asked her to return the boy to his mother. Satyavati asks to see Urvashi, so that she may return her son to her. Urvashi is summoned, and seeing her son, embraces him with joy. Satyavati takes her leave and, promising to send the young prince's pet peacock to him, returns to the hermitage.

The king is overcome with joy, but Urvashi begins to weep. She explains to the king how, by Indra's decree, she could stay with him only till he should see the face of their son, and how, afraid of being parted from him, she had hidden their child away; now that he had seen the face of his son, she had to return to Indra. The heartbroken king, unable to contemplate a life without Urvashi, decides to hand over his kingdom to his son and leave for an ascetic existence in the forest.

Just then, the divine sage Narada arrives in a flash of lightning with a message from Indra to the king. A war between the gods and the danavas has been foretold, says the message, and therefore the king, who is Indra's ally and comrade in arms, must not lay down his weapons so soon. The message goes on to say that Urvashi would stay by his side as his lawful wife till the end of his life on earth. Pururava and Urvashi are relieved and grateful, Prince Ayush is anointed the heir apparent, and tragedy is averted. The play ends on a note of joyful contentment.

Inspiration for 'Vikramorvashiyam'

The story of Urvashi and Pururava is an ancient one, told and retold over millennia in myth and literature. It is first mentioned in the *Rigveda*, composed sometime during the second millennium BCE. Later versions of the tale are found in the *Shatapatha Brahmana*, in the *Mahabharata*, the Puranas, and in the tales of the *Brihatkatha*. The story has changed considerably over time, as stories often do, reaching its most pleasing form in Kalidasa's play.

The *Rigveda* consists of more than a thousand suktas or songs in praise of various gods arranged in 10 mandalas or books; the suktas are made up of riks or verses. A sukta is referenced by its number, and the number of the mandala in which it occurs. It is in the last and final book of the *Rigveda* (RV), in Sukta 10.95, that we first find the story of Urvashi and Pururava. The sukta consists of 18 verses. The first 17 of these are in the form of a somewhat fraught exchange between Urvashi and Pururava. The following summary of the sukta is based on the translation and explanation given by McComas Taylor in his essay 'Lambs, Lightning, Nakedness and Fire: Polythetic Networks and Literary Elaborations of the Purūravas–Urvaśī Narrative'.

It is clear from their conversation that Urvashi, angered by Pururava's disrespectful behaviour towards her, has left him, and that he has come in search of her. He reminds her of their happy life together and asks her to return. But Urvashi has no such memories and tells him to go back home. The king becomes preoccupied with thoughts of the other apsaras, so Urvashi reminds him about their son Ayu, saying that these very apsaras were present at his birth.

At the thought of his son, Pururava again asks her to come back to him. But Urvashi is adamant in her refusal and offers, instead, to send the child to him. Pururava then takes recourse to manipulation, saying that if he leaves for some far distant place, he might die. This has the desired effect, and Urvashi's anger begins to fade. She begs him not to go away, not to die, but she also reminds him of the hardships she faced in their four years together. Pururava responds with tenderness, asking her to come back to him. The last stanza is spoken by a narrator who addresses Pururava as the son of Ila and reminds him that the gods have said that he will die like a mortal, that his descendants will conduct fire-sacrifices in honour of the gods, and that eventually he will reach Indra's heaven. Though Kalidasa's Urvashi and Pururava are very different from their ancient counterparts, their story is rooted in the Rigvedic tale.

Sukta 10.95 gives neither context nor backstory for the conversation between Urvashi and Pururava, nor any explanation for the narrator's statements. This lack of background information is a common feature of most Rigvedic sutras. The songs, composed by priest–poets for use during elaborate fire-sacrifices, were often intentionally obscure and usually assumed that all those involved in a ritual performance would already have the knowledge necessary to understand them. As time passed, the precise meanings of the Rigvedic suktas began to be lost. As they grew more and more difficult to understand, commentaries to explain the songs and associated rituals began to be composed.

One of the earliest of these commentaries was the *Shatapatha Brahmana* (SB); attributed to the sage

Yajnavalkya, it was composed sometime during the seventh or sixth centuries BCE. In this is included an interpretation of the Urvashi–Pururava dialogue contained in the *Rigveda*. The explanation provides a context for the conversation in RV 10.95 and a backstory that helps make sense of the sukta. It is given briefly here, based, once again, on the summary given by McComas Taylor in his essay.

According to the *Shatapatha Brahmana*, Urvashi falls in love with Pururava and marries him on two conditions: that he never makes love to her without her consent, and that she never sees him unclothed. They live together in the mortal world for many years, and Urvashi becomes pregnant with his child. The gandharvas, who missed her presence, now decide she has lived in the mortal world long enough, and scheme to get her back.

As it happens, Urvashi has a pet ewe which she keeps, along with its two lambs, tied to her bed. One night, as she lies asleep with Pururava, the gandharvas steal first one lamb and then the other. Both times Urvashi cries out, calling for a hero to save her lambs. The second time, Pururava jumps out of bed, thinking to catch the thieves; not wanting to waste time, he does not stop to put on any clothes. In that instant the gandharvas cause a flash of lightning. Urvashi sees Pururava naked and immediately vanishes.

Pururava, weeping in sorrow, wanders all over the land searching for her till at last he comes to a large lake, where several apsaras, including Urvashi, are swimming about in the form of waterbirds. Urvashi, seeing him, takes on human form and Pururava recognizes her. According to the *Shatapatha Brahmana*, it is at this point in the story that the dialogue described in RV 10.95 takes place. However, the tone and tenor of their conversation is gentler here.

As in the Rigvedic verse, Pururava asks her to return, but she refuses, saying she cannot since he failed to do as she had asked. The *Shatapatha Brahmana* now adds to the tale. Urvashi asks Pururava to return a year later, promising that he could then be with her and a son would be born to him. Pururava does so, and on Urvashi's advice, asks the gandharvas for a boon – that he become one of them. The gandharvas grant him his wish. They give him the sacred fire and say that by using this for sacrifice, he would become one of them. Pururava leaves with his son and the sacred fire. The rest of the tale is taken up by how he brings the sacred fire to the world of mortals. Finally, by performing a sacrifice with that sacred fire, he becomes one of the gandharvas. The story given in the *Shatapatha Brahmana* became foundational, and elements from it are present in most later versions of the tale.

The story of Urvashi and Pururava is also found in the *Mahabharata*. The epic probably reached its present form during the fourth century CE. In the first of its 18 books, it is related that Pururava, son of Ila, was the one who brought down the sacred fire from the region of the gandharvas to the world of mortals. He also brought from there the apsara Urvashi, from whom he had six sons, the eldest of whom was called Ayush. There is no mention here of Pururava's separation from Urvashi or their subsequent reunion. The Urvashi–Pururava story also occurs in the *Harivamsha* (Genealogy of Hari), a text often regarded as an appendix to the *Mahabharata*. The tale as given in this text more or less follows the Vedic tale in the *Shatapatha Brahmana*, with some additions and amendments. The date of the *Harivamsha* is uncertain – it was probably composed between the second and fourth centuries CE but contains material that may be dated as far back as the second century BCE.

A version of the Urvashi–Pururava story is found in the *Matsyapurana*, one of the earliest of several collections of ancient myths and legends known collectively as the Puranas. Traditionally, there are 18 major Puranas, the earliest of which were composed between 200 and 750 CE. The Puranas were constantly revised and updated, and therefore contain stories much older than the date of their final compilation. The date of the *Matsyapurana* is uncertain, but it is likely that the text reached its final form between 250 and 500 CE. The *Matsyapurana* version of the story is given briefly below; it is based on the summaries given in McComas Taylor's essay and in M.R. Kale's introduction to his translation of Kalidasa's *Vikramorvashiyam*.

According to the *Matsyapurana* story, Pururava, the son of Budha and Ila, was a mighty king who performed a hundred ashvamedhas; through Vishnu's favour, he became the ruler of the whole world. Once, Dharma, Artha, and Kama (virtue, wealth, and love, the three goals of human existence) became curious to see which of them the king revered most. So they took on bodily form and came to visit him. Pururava greeted them all with great respect, but he paid extra homage to Dharma. This offended Artha and Kama. Artha decreed that greed would be his downfall, and Kama declared that he would be separated from his bride and go mad in the sacred grove of Kumara on the Gandhamadana mountain. But Dharma declared that he would live a long and virtuous life, and that his descendants would rule the earth as long as the sun and moon endured. So saying, the three deities disappeared.

Now Pururava used to visit Indra every day. Once, mounted on his chariot and on his way to visit the god, he saw the danava Keshi kidnap and carry away the apsaras

Chitralekha and Urvashi. Pururava fought the danava, killed him with his arrow, and rescued the apsaras. He also restored Indra to his throne, which the danava had threatened. In return, Indra acknowledged him as his friend and ally, and gave him even more glory, wealth, and power.

One day, Indra invited Pururava to his realm to watch a play, the creation of the sage Bharata, depicting Lakshmi's svayamvara. Indra commanded the apsaras Menaka, Rambha, and Urvashi to play their given roles. But Urvashi, distracted by the king's presence, forgot her lines. This angered the sage so much that he condemned her to be separated from the king on earth, and, transformed into a vine, pine for him for 55 years. Urvashi married the king and lived with him on earth; and after the sage's curse had been fulfilled, she bore him eight sons, the eldest of whom was called Ayush.

It is evident that the *Matsyapurana* version is very close to the story of Kalidasa's play. Versions of the tale are also found in several of the other Puranas. It is given in great detail in the *Vishnupurana*, where, with a few additions, it follows closely the Vedic tale given in the *Shatapatha Brahmana*. The version contained in the *Padmapurana* is almost identical to that in the *Matsyapurana*.

A somewhat different version of the Urvashi–Pururava story is found in the fourth-century collection of ancient tales known as the *Brihatkatha*. The collection is now lost, and its tales, well known in Kalidasa's time, are available to us only through later retellings such as the eleventh-century *Kathasaritsagara* by Somadeva. The story in the *Kathasaritsagara* is told by Udayana, king of Vatsa, as a parallel to his own separation from his queen Vasavadatta. In this version, Pururava is a devotee of Vishnu.

One day, while strolling in Indra's pleasure garden, Pururava catches sight of the apsara Urvashi, and both are smitten with love for each other. Vishnu, realizing the state of the king's heart, sends Narada to Indra, asking the latter to unite Urvashi and Pururava. Indra does so, and the lovers live happily together for a while. One day, a war breaks out between Indra and the danavas. Indra asks Pururava for assistance, and, with his help, wins the war.

In the celebrations that follow, Pururava sees the apsara Rambha dancing and laughs. Rambha is affronted, and when she questions his knowledge of the dance she was performing, he replies that by being with Urvashi he knew dances which even her teacher, the gandharva Tumburu, did not know. Tumburu is enraged to hear the king's remark and curses him to be separated from Urvashi till he propitiates Vishnu. Pururava returns to Earth and Urvashi is carried away by the gandharvas. Pururava performs penance till Vishnu is appeased. The gandharvas then return Urvashi to him, and the reunited lovers resume their life together.

It is likely that Kalidasa was familiar with several, if not all, of these sources. Regardless of the source or sources he used, he has adapted this ancient story into an intense and pleasing drama.

Commentaries

The two known commentators on *Vikramorvashiyam* are Katayavema and Ranganatha.

Katayavema was minister to the Reddi king Kumaragiri (reigned 1386–1402 CE) of Kondavidu (in present-day Andhra Pradesh). He therefore calls his commentary

Kumaragirirajiya. He has commented on all three plays of Kalidasa. In the initial stanzas of his commentary on *Abhijnanashakuntalam*, he tells us that his name was Vema, his father's name was Kata, and that Kataya was the name of an ancestor of his.

Ranganatha, in the concluding stanza of his work, tells us that he wrote his commentary in Vikrami Samvat 1712 (1656 CE). His commentary contains a more elaborate version of the play. However, he is not always regarded as reliable.

Adaptations and Translations

Over the last 200 years, *Vikramorvashiyam* has been translated several times into English and major Indian languages. These include Bengali, Gujarati, Hindi, Kannada, Maithili, Malayalam, Marathi, Odia, Tamil, Telugu, and Urdu. It has also been translated into Persian. More recent translations into English include David Gitomer's *Urvashi Won by Valor* (Theater of Memory, 1984); Chandra Rajan's *Vikram and Urvashi* (2002); and A.N.D. Haksar's *Vikramorvashiyam: Quest for Urvashi* (2021).

A Glimpse into 'Vikramorvashiyam'

From Act 4

Selected verses addressed by the king to various forest creatures.

The king, driven mad by Urvashi's sudden disappearance, searches for her throughout the forest, and asks every creature he sees for news of her.

To the peacock

O peacock, I beg of you,
tell me please, if you did see
my loved one roaming in this forest.
She is like the moon at night
and has a swan-like gait:
you will know her by these signs
told to you by me. 20

O blue-necked bird, my anxious longing
for that long-eyed and fair-limbed maid,
who, if in this forest was seen by you,
would be a favour to my sight. 21

To the koel

O sweet-singing cuckoo, dear,
tell me if she was seen by you,
my sweetheart roaming by herself
in the garden of paradise. 24

Lovers do call you Kama's emissary,
his weapon immaculate, and an expert
at breaking down the other's pride:
so, bring my darling close to me,
or lead me, you sweet-voice, to where she is. 25

To swans flying overhead to the Manasa lake

O mountain birds,
Before you fly away to that lake,
do drop those lotus stalks you carry,
and pick up others again,
But rescue me from this distress
with some news of my beloved:
good folks listen to others too
before minding their own interests. 31

If, O swan, you did not see
my darling with her curving brows
pass by on that lake's shore,
O thief, how did you then acquire
her playful but stately gait? 32

To the bee

O bee, you would praise the ways
of my darling with her eyes like wine,
but have not yet beheld her person.

If you had the fragrance smelt
of the breath pervading from her lips,
would you still love this white lotus? 42

To the elephant

O great elephant, who can break
big trees with a playful blow,
please tell me, as I ask of you,
did you see my love passing by,
she, whose glow outshines the moon. 45

O rutting lord of the elephant herd,
did you have the pleasure of a glimpse
of that woman in her prime of youth,
her hair with jasmine flowers strung,
gleaming like a crescent moon
that may be seen from far? 46

To the deer

O lord of the deer folk,
was my beloved seen by you
in this forest? I will tell you
her distinctive features, listen:
she has large eyes, just like your mate,
and looks just as beautiful. 60

– from *Vikramorvashiyam: Quest for Urvashi*,
translated by A.N.D Haksar

'Abhijnanashakuntalam' or The Recognition of Shakuntala

Abhijnanashakuntalam is the last of Kalidasa's three plays. It is his finest and probably final work. The play is a mix of myth and fairy tale, magic and romance, and relates in seven acts the ancient story of Dushyanta, king of Hastinapur, and Shakuntala, the adopted daughter of the sage Kanva. The plot is drawn primarily from the *Mahabharata*, and though the story is well-known, Kalidasa imbues it with a sensitivity and poignancy missing in the tale as told in the epic. His language is elegant in its simplicity, evocative, musical, and nuanced, his use of literary devices dexterous and accomplished, his characters finely drawn. In short, the play is polished perfection, sufficient in itself to place Kalidasa first among the ancient dramatists, unsurpassed by any other.

Title

The Sanskrit word *abhijnanam* is defined as 'recognition' by the lexicographer V.S. Apte in his Sanskrit–English dictionary. Additional meanings given by Apte include 'remembrance, recollection; knowledge, ascertainment' and 'a sign or token of recognition'. The word *abhijnana*, explains Apte, is 'a combination of *anubhava* or direct perception and *smriti* or recollection', or 'a sort of direct perception assisted by the memory'. The title, thus means, quite literally, 'the recognition or knowing of Shakuntala'. It is an apt title, at first glance almost an obvious one – Dushyanta loses his memory thanks to Durvasa's curse, and it is only when he sees his ring, the abhijnana or 'token of recognition', that he remembers Shakuntala.

The title also points to the question we find ourselves asking throughout the play: 'Does Dushyanta really know Shakuntala for who she is?' In the beginning, he is attracted to her beauty and quickly marries her, but beyond the physical intimacy of their relationship, he barely knows her. As Chandra Rajan writes in her introduction to Kalidasa's plays, she is more a beautiful object than a person to him, an object that he, as king, has taken for himself as he might a precious jewel or a flower. It is much later, after his memory returns, that he begins to think about her as his wife and the mother of his child; he truly 'recognizes' her only at the end of the play.

Setting

The play is set in a lost and distant past, when gods and heroes walked the earth. The action takes place in several locations.

The first four acts, which constitute more than half the play, take place in the hermitage of Kanva or in the surrounding forests of the Himalayan foothills. This is the quiet and secluded world in which Shakuntala grew up. The next two acts take place in the royal city of Hastinapura, in its bustling marketplace and the king's bejewelled palace. This is Dushyanta's world of power, wealth, and politics. The final act takes place in the celestial sphere, along the heavenly paths in the sky, and then in the hermitage of the sage Maricha upon Hemakuta, the golden mountain range that is home to the kinnaras, heavenly singers in the service of Kubera, the god of wealth.

Structure

The play consists of seven acts, arranged in careful and deliberate symmetry. The story of Shakuntala and Dushyanta may be divided into two parts: their meeting and union (Acts 1–3) and their separation and reunion (Acts 5–7). Act 4, placed in the centre, contains the pivotal episode of Durvasa's curse, which leads to the future separation of the lovers. Thus, Act 4 separates the two parts of the play from each other, but in providing the causal connection between the first part and the second part, it also brings the two separate parts together, unifying the play into a coherent whole. (A more detailed analysis of this inherent symmetry in *Abhijnanashakuntalam* is given by M.R. Kale in the introduction to his translation of the play.)

It is worth noting that the entire incident of the curse, despite its momentous nature, is presented only as a prelude in Act 4, and Durvasa himself, despite his key role in the lives of the lovers, never appears before the audience but is only heard offstage.

The play begins with the traditional prologue; after the invocation to Shiva, the sutradhara introduces the play as a new drama composed by Kalidasa. He also states that the play is being performed in summer, which is also the season during which the opening scenes of the drama occur. The play ends with the customary Bharatavakya or epilogue.

Kalidasa uses 24 musical metres across the play, in particular the metre known as the Arya.

Characters

The hero or nayaka of the play is King Dushyanta of the lunar dynasty, ruler of Hastinapur. He is endowed with every kingly quality, and is revered in all the worlds for his moral integrity and nobility of mind. He is brave, handsome, youthful, and well-spoken, with a refined and sensitive understanding of the arts, particularly painting. He is also a skilled warrior, and the friend and ally of Indra, king of the gods. While we are aware that he is a great and powerful ruler, we see him, like Pururava in *Vikramorvashiyam*, chiefly in the role of a lover. His consort is Queen Vasumati. He is also referred to as Duhshanta in some recensions of the play.

The heroine or nayika of the play is Shakuntala, adopted daughter of the sage Kanva. She is an exceedingly beautiful young woman; sheltered from the wider world, she is modest and innocent, but also spirited enough to stand up for herself when unjustly accused of dishonesty and deceit by Dushyanta. Her real parents are the sage Vishvamitra and the apsara Menaka. The sage was born a Kshatriya, of the warrior class, but by practising intense austerities, he raised himself to the Brahmana or priestly class and became one of the seven great rishis. Once, as he sat by the River Gautami engaged in rigorous penance, the gods, afraid of the power he would acquire through his austerities, sent the apsara Menaka to seduce him and disrupt his austerities; this she successfully accomplished. The result of their union was their daughter Shakuntala. Menaka abandoned Shakuntala as soon as she was born and left her in the forest where she was fed and looked after by birds. The rishi Kanva found and rescued the abandoned child and brought her up as his own daughter.

Kanva is an important character in the play. He is the head of his hermitage, and revered for his asceticism and the power that his austerities have conferred upon him. He is also a wise and practical man, and an affectionate father to his adopted daughter.

Kalidasa does not forget Shakuntala's semi-divine origin – she is, after all, the daughter of an apsara, and, like her mother, closely associated with Nature – and portrays her almost in the form of a woodland spirit. The trees are her kin, the flowers her sisters, and the animals her especial charge.

Shakuntala's son by Dushyanta is the child Sarvadamana; in myth, literature, and legend, he grows up to be the illustrious emperor Bharata.

The vidushaka Madhavya is the king's close friend and companion. His female counterparts are Anasuya and Priyamvada, Shakuntala's companions in the hermitage and her dearest friends; they are devoted to Shakuntala.

An important character is the sage Durvasa. Quick to take offence and easily angered, he is responsible for the curse that causes the separation of Shakuntala and Dushyanta. Despite his critical role in their story, he remains offstage, the audience merely hearing his voice from behind the curtain.

Bards and musicians sing and play offstage. Voices of deities, divinities, and woodland spirits are also heard speaking and singing offstage.

The sage Maricha and his consort Aditi appear only in the final act. According to the *Mahabharata*, the sage is the son of Marichi (Brahma's son), and the father of all humankind. He is married to Aditi (and her 12 sisters). From Aditi were born the gods and humankind, and from his other wives were born all other living beings, including the danavas. The sage is also known by the name Kashyapa and is referred to as such in some recensions of the play.

Other characters include Matali, Indra's charioteer; Somarata, Dushyanta's preceptor and royal priest; the ascetics Sharngarava, Sharadvata, and Gautami; the apsara Mishrakeshi (called Sanumati in some recensions); and the fisherman and policemen in Hastinapura.

Characters who are mentioned in the play but do not appear on stage include Vasumati, Dushyanta's consort and chief queen; Vishvamitra and Menaka, Shakuntala's real parents; Indra, king of the gods, and his son Jayanta; and Dhanamitra (Dhanavriddhi in some recensions), a wealthy merchant of Hastinapura, lost at sea.

Summary

Act 1 is set in the forests of the Himalayan foothills, and in the hermitage of the sage Kanva by the banks of the River Malini. The season is summer.

As the prologue comes to an end, the sutradhara draws the audience's attention to King Dushyanta pursuing a deer. The sutradhara exits, and the king enters on his chariot with his charioteer; he is in full hunting gear and armed with a bow and arrows. As he is about to shoot the deer he is chasing, a voice offstage commands him to stop, for the deer must not be killed. The king and his charioteer see a group of ascetics barring their way. They explain that the deer belongs to the hermitage of the sage Kanva and request him to put away his arrow. The king graciously complies, and the pleased ascetics invite him to the hermitage. They explain that the sage himself is away, but his daughter Shakuntala is there and would most certainly receive him with the hospitality due a guest.

The king accepts the invitation and makes his way to the hermitage. Asking his charioteer to wait outside, he goes in and sees three young women watering the shrubs and plants. He realizes they are Kanva's daughter Shakuntala and her friends Anasuya and Priyamvada. He is captivated by Shakuntala's beauty and stands where he is, watching the young women and listening to their conversation. He hopes fervently that she is Kanva's daughter by a wife not of the priestly class, for only then would she be able to marry a man of the warrior class to which he, the king, belongs. He decides to find out more about her.

Meanwhile, Shakuntala is chased by a bee, and her friends, laughing, refuse to help, saying she should call out to the king for help, since the hermitage was under his protection. At this, Dushyanta steps forward to help, startling the young women who had so far been oblivious of his presence.

Recovering, the young women welcome him to the hermitage and sit with him to keep him company. Shakuntala is as captivated by him as he with her, and longs to know more about him. But, even upon being asked directly by Anasuya, Dushyanta does not reveal that he is the king but pretends instead to be a minister in his own court. He, however, manages to find out more about Shakuntala's parentage, and learns that her real parents are the sage Vishvamitra and the apsara Menaka. Since her natural father Vishvamitra is a royal sage of the warrior class just as he, Dushyanta, is himself, this makes Shakuntala also of the warrior class and a suitable bride for him.

Just then, news comes of a wild elephant that, terrified by the sight of a chariot, has run amok. The king and the young women rise in alarm. Shakuntala's friends leave; Shakuntala finds excuses to linger but finally follows her friends. The king leaves as well; he is no longer in a hurry to return to Hastinapur and decides to set up camp close to the hermitage. The Act ends with his exit.

Act 2 is set in the surrounding forest. It begins on the morning of the day after the events depicted in Act 1.

The vidushaka, Madhavya, enters. He is disgruntled, dejected, and fed up of the king's passion for hunting – as the king's friend and constant companion, he is required to accompany him on every expedition, and has had enough of the inconveniences he therefore has to face. Besides, there seems no prospect of returning to the comforts of the city because the king has fallen in love with a hermit girl! He sees the king approaching and takes up a tired, drooping stance in the hope of garnering sympathy from the king. But Dushyanta is immersed in thoughts of Shakuntala and barely notices his vidushaka's state. Madhavya complains that the king has forgotten all his royal duties and is camped out in the wilderness with no regard for Madhavya's bruised and aching limbs. He begs the king to call a day's break in the hunting.

The king smilingly agrees, for the vidushaka had expressed his own desire: the king no longer wants to hunt the deer so loved by Shakuntala or kill any animals in the vicinity of the hermitage. He uses Madhavya's grumbling to order his general to stop the hunt and orders his troops to leave the animals in peace. The attendants are dismissed, and the king, now alone with Madhavya, tells him about his love for Shakuntala.

Madhavya tries to dissuade him, but the king is not to be deflected. He explains her parentage to him and how, therefore, he may marry her by law and social convention. He holds forth at length upon her unparalleled beauty, and relates how, as she was leaving with her friends, she had made an excuse to stay, thus showing her true feelings. He asks Madhavya to find a way for him to enter the hermitage again without arousing suspicion.

Just then, ascetics arrive from the hermitage. They explain that in the absence of Kanva, the daityas, mortal enemies of the gods, will begin disturbing their sacrificial rites. They request that the king with his charioteer stay for a few days in the hermitage to protect their rites from these demons. The king agrees with alacrity. But, as he prepares to leave for the hermitage, a messenger arrives from his mother, requesting his immediate presence by her side to fulfil the requirements of a fast she is keeping. The king is torn in two; after some thought, he decides to send the vidushaka in his stead to the capital. Madhavya, says the king, could explain to his royal mother his obligation to help the hermitage, and also stand in as her son for the rituals associated with the fast.

Madhavya, in addition to his complaints about forest life, is also afraid of the demons. He agrees without protest to return to the capital. Dushyanta, suddenly worried that Madhavya, who could be quite indiscreet, might inadvertently tell his queen and the ladies in his harem of his passion for Shakuntala, tells him that all that he had said about her had been in joke and was not to be taken seriously. Madhavya and the king leave; this ends Act 2.

Act 3 is located in Kanva's hermitage and in a shady bower by the banks of the Malini. The action takes place perhaps a fortnight or so after the events of Act 2. It is still summer.

The act opens with a prelude in which the audience learn that Dushyanta – who has now been recognized as the king – has successfully protected the sacrificial rites from the demons. It is also stated that Shakuntala has fallen ill with heatstroke and is being treated with cooling remedies by Priyamvada and Anasuya; the audience, of course, can surmise that she has fallen in love with Dushyanta, and her real affliction is not heatstroke but passion.

As the prelude ends, the king enters, in the throes of love. He walks about, sighing pensively and thinking about his beloved, and decides to go towards the river where he assumes that Shakuntala and her friends have taken refuge against the heat of the midday sun. He finds the three young women resting in a bower.

Shakuntala is clearly in distress, and, when questioned by her friends, confesses that she has fallen in love with the king. Dushyanta, unseen by the young women, listens to their conversation with delight. Priyamvada suggests that Shakuntala compose a letter to the king, which she will somehow convey to him. Anasuya agrees and, together with Priyamvada, urges Shakuntala to write down her feelings for the king. Shakuntala does so, and as she reads aloud the song she has composed, the king steps forward. Priyamvada and Anasuya greet him joyfully and, making up an excuse, leave the lovers alone.

Dushyanta and Shakuntala confess their feelings to each other, and Dushyanta reassures her of his intentions towards her. They are interrupted by the voice of Gautami, an elderly female ascetic in the hermitage, who has come to inquire after Shakuntala's state of health. The king quickly hides, and Gautami enters, full of concern for Shakuntala. It is evening now, and Gautami takes Shakuntala away with her. The king, disconsolate at the parting, is also called away by the ascetics to guard their evening rituals. This brings Act 3 to a close.

Act 4 is set in Kanva's hermitage. It opens with a prelude, which takes place a few days after the events in Act 3. Summer has come to an end, and it is the first day of the rainy season. Priyamvada and Anasuya enter, gathering flowers for worship. We learn from their conversation that since the events of the last act, the king has married Shakuntala by the gandharva rite. This is a form of marriage based on a mutual declaration of love between a man and woman without any formal ceremony or witnesses; the lovers do not need permission from parents or family. We also learn that the king has completed his duties at the hermitage and, after promising to send for Shakuntala, has left for his capital city.

As Priyamvada and Anasuya continue to gather flowers, the voice of a guest, announcing his arrival at the hermitage, is heard offstage. Shakuntala is in the hermitage but, immersed in thoughts of Dushyanta, she fails to greet the guest. Unfortunately for her, the guest is the hot-tempered sage Durvasa. Furious at the perceived slight, Durvasa pronounces a curse upon Shakuntala; he is heard offstage, decreeing that she, neglecting to receive him properly, will be forgotten by the very person of whom she is thinking, that he will not remember her even when reminded by her.

Anasuya and Priyamvada are horrified to see Durvasa, shaking with anger, striding off in the distance. Anasuya runs after the sage and pleads with him to forgive Shakuntala. Durvasa relents; unable to take back his words, he concedes that the curse will be broken the moment Shakuntala presents the king with a token of recognition. Priyamvada and Anasuya console themselves with this concession, for they remember that Dushyanta had slipped his signet ring upon Shakuntala's finger at parting; the ring also had his name inscribed upon it. Since a token of recognition was easily available, they decide not to tell anyone about the curse, not even Shakuntala, as it would be too much of a shock for her. This ends the prelude.

The remainder of Act 4 takes place five to six months later. The rainy season has come to an end, and it is now autumn. Shakuntala is pregnant with Dushyanta's child. However, Durvasa's curse has begun to take effect for, despite his promise, the king has still not sent for her. The sage Kanva has returned to the hermitage, where he learns of Shakuntala's marriage with Dushyanta and gives his approval. He decides to send her to her husband's home.

The rest of the act is taken up with the preparations for Shakuntala's departure. The trees of the forest provide silken garments for her to wear, and woodland spirits present her with precious jewels. She bids a tearful farewell to the plants and animals she had cared for, and to the little orphaned fawn she had brought up like a son and who does not want to let her go. She takes leave of her beloved father, who is as tearful as she is at the parting. Priyamvada and Anasuya, secretly worried about the curse, tell her to show Dushyanta his ring if he has any trouble recognizing her. This alarms Shakuntala, but her friends reassure her, saying they are just anxious out of love for her. She leaves, accompanied by Gautami, and the ascetics Sharngarava and Sharadvata. Act 4 ends as all the characters exit.

The action now moves to the king's capital, Hastinapura. It is still autumn.

Act 5 takes place in Dushyanta's palace. After a few days of travel, Shakuntala and the ascetics reach the city and make their way to the palace. The king, having finished with his court and affairs of state for the day, is relaxing with his friend, the vidushaka Madhavya. He is listening to a love song one of his junior queens, Hamsavati, is singing offstage, reproaching him for his neglect of her. His chamberlain, Parvatayana, announces the arrival of the ascetics, saying that they have come from Kanva's hermitage and there are women with them. The king clearly has no memory of Shakuntala and cannot think why any ascetics should be visiting him. Puzzled and curious, he asks the visitors to be shown in.

The ascetics and Shakuntala are led in. The king is moved by Shakuntala's loveliness and by a feeling he can't quite explain, but, believing her to be another's wife, he looks away. When the sages present her to him as his bride and asks him to accept her as his queen, he is taken aback and denies that he knows her. Gautami removes Shakuntala's veil, in the hope that the king will recognize her. Though moved once more by her beauty, he cannot remember her; seeing that she is clearly pregnant, and unable to recall marrying her, he refuses to accept her.

Shakuntala, hurt and angry, accuses him of perfidy and deceit, and offers to show him a token by which he will recognize her. The king agrees, but she cannot find his ring. She realizes that it must have slipped off her finger during the journey. She attempts to jog the king's memory by relating an incident only he knew had happened. But Dushyanta cannot remember it; it is now his turn to accuse her of deceit and he declares that she is trying to foist another man's unborn child upon him. This is the final straw for Shakuntala; she bursts out in anger, calling him cruel, ignoble, a cheat, and a liar, and weeps at the fate that made her fall into his trap. The ascetics are equally angry at the king's behaviour; declaring that Shakuntala was his true wife and so it was up to him to accept or abandon her, they prepare to leave.

Shakuntala is distraught at being abandoned by both the king and the ascetics. Somarata, the royal priest, is also present at this scene. He steps in, offering Shakuntala shelter in his own home till she gives birth. If, he says, the child has all the marks of greatness, as has been predicted for Dushyanta's son, then Shakuntala should be accepted by the king; if not, she should be sent back to her father. The king and the ascetics accept this solution. The ascetics leave the king's audience hall. Shakuntala follows the royal priest, weeping, and calling to the goddess Earth to swallow her up. The king is left behind, pondering this strange incident.

A voice is heard exclaiming in wonder offstage. Somarata, the royal priest, enters. He explains what has just occurred: Shakuntala, he says, has been carried away by an apsara from the celestial realm. The king and his attendants cannot explain what has happened. The king retires, his mind and heart troubled by the events of that afternoon. This ends Act 5.

As the audience would have guessed, the apsara who carries Shakuntala away is her mother, Menaka. Shakuntala's distress, her calling upon the goddess Earth for help, and

being rescued by her mother are reminiscent of Sita's distress in the *Ramayana* – when asked by Rama to prove her chastity a second time, she calls upon her mother, the Earth, to take her away, and the Earth opens and swallows her. Kalidasa's audience would have been fully aware of the parallel.

Act 6 takes place in Hastinapura, some five or six years after the events in Act 5. The season is spring.

The act begins in a marketplace in Hastinapura. We learn that the king's signet ring has been found inside a fish by a fisherman. The man is accused of stealing the ring; he is arrested and taken to the palace for the king to give his verdict. He is, of course, freed by the king, who recognizes his ring. The king, upon seeing the ring, is also freed from Durvasa's curse. The prelude ends here.

The scene now moves to the pleasure gardens of the king's palace. A few days have passed since the discovery of the ring. A pair of gardeners is working in the pleasure groves. An apsara called Mishrakeshi flies in. She is a friend of Shakuntala's mother, Menaka, who has requested her to keep an eye on Dushyanta. Unseen by the others, Mishrakeshi eavesdrops on the gardeners' conversation. The king has regained his memory. He can now remember Shakuntala and his marriage with her but, helpless to find her, he is sunk in grief and has forbidden the celebration of the spring festival.

The king enters, accompanied by Madhavya. Despite the vidushaka's attempts to distract him, Dushyanta can think and speak only of Shakuntala. As he sits in the garden, admiring a half-finished portrait of Shakuntala that he is painting, he hears that his chief queen, Vasumati, is on her way to see him. Madhavya hurries away with Shakuntala's portrait. But the queen, seeing official documents from the chief minister being carried in to the king, changes her mind. The documents state that a wealthy merchant called Dhanamitra has died in a shipwreck, and that, since he was childless and has left no heir, his property has become part of the royal treasury. This causes a fresh upsurge of grief in the king as he remembers his own childless state, and his repudiation of Shakuntala when she was so clearly pregnant. He falls unconscious with the intensity of his sorrow. Mishrakeshi, watching and listening, is reassured of the king's affection for Shakuntala, and flies off to give the good news to her friend, Menaka.

Just then a great commotion breaks out offstage. It is Madhavya, seemingly calling for help. The king regains consciousness with a start. He calls for his weapons, but just then Matali, Indra's charioteer, enters with Madhavya, who is quite uninjured. Matali is amused at Madhavya's panic at his arrival, and, greeting the king, gives him Indra's message to join him in battle against the danavas. Dushyanta leaves with Matali in Indra's chariot. This brings Act 6 to a close.

Act 7 is set in the celestial realm and takes place shortly after the events in Act 6.

The act begins with Matali and Dushyanta who, mounted on Indra's chariot, are on their way back to Earth. We learn from their conversation that Dushyanta has successfully defeated the danavas and has been honoured by Indra with a garland of mandara flowers. The king admires the view of the earth, spread below them, from Indra's chariot. In the distance he sees a mountain range, its peaks glowing red and gold. Matali informs him that the range is known as Hemakuta, the home of the celestial singers, the kinnaras; upon this peak lies the hermitage of the sage Maricha and his consort Aditi. The king decides to stop at the hermitage to pay his respects to the great sage.

While Matali leaves to find Maricha, Dushyanta sees a young boy in the care of two ascetic women. The child, who is addressed as Sarvadamana by the women, is playing with a lion cub. Dushyanta is overcome with affection for him, as though the child were his own son. The wayward child refuses to let go of the lion cub, and the ascetic women appeal for the king's help. As the king goes up to the child, the women exclaim at the likeness between the two, and the king learns that the boy belongs to the Puru lineage (which is also his own) and that his mother's name is Shakuntala. He suspects that the child is, in truth, his own.

The women notice in alarm that the protective amulet the child wears on his wrist has fallen off. The king sees it lying upon the ground and picks it up. The women warn him not to touch it, but, too late, the king is already holding it in his hand. They explain that the amulet was given to the child by Maricha, and that if it falls off his wrist, it may not be picked up by any except his parents or the child himself; if others were to pick it up, it would turn into a snake and bite them. The women, now realizing that it was the king himself who had picked up the charm, hurry away to inform Shakuntala.

Shakuntala enters, almost afraid to believe that the king has come to the hermitage. The two recognize each other, and the king falls at Shakuntala's feet and begs her to forgive him. The lovers are reconciled. She sees the signet ring upon his finger, and he explains that it was the sight of the ring that brought his memory back.

Just then, Matali returns and, after congratulating the king on his reunion with Shakuntala, says that the sage Maricha would now see him. He leads Dushyanta, Shakuntala, and their son to where sits Maricha, attended by Aditi. Maricha tells them of Durvasa's curse and explains to the king that his repudiation of Shakuntala was not his fault. The king breathes a sigh of relief, and Shakuntala, till now unaware of the curse, understands why her friends had asked her to show Dushyanta the ring.

Maricha prophesies that their son, Sarvadamana, will become a great king and, by his protection of the world, he will acquire the name 'Bharata' ('the protector'). The sage then sends a disciple to Kanva with the news that Shakuntala and her son have been reunited with Dushyanta. The play ends as Maricha blesses the king and bids him return to his capital, driving Indra's chariot and accompanied by his wife and son.

Inspiration for 'Abhijnanashakuntalam'

The earliest mention of Shakuntala is found in the *Shatapatha Brahmana*, a prose commentary on the Vedas composed sometime during the seventh or sixth centuries BCE. A single line in the thirteenth book of the text states: 'At Nadapit the Apsara Shakuntala conceived Bharata.' The *Shatapatha Brahmana* refers to Bharata as 'Dauhshanti', or 'son of Duhshanta (Dushyanta)'. It also states that Bharata 'after conquering the whole earth, brought to Indra more than a thousand horses, meet for sacrifice' and that 'the greatness of Bharata' remained unrivalled – this is in line with Maricha's prophecy for the child Sarvadamana.

The story is not given in any detail in the text, but the various references to it indicate that it was well known in Vedic times. Unfortunately, this ancient version of the tale has been lost to us.

A long and tedious version of the story is found in the first book of the *Mahabharata* (c. fourth century BCE). Though quite unromantic, this version of the story is probably the basis for Kalidasa's play. The story in the epic, summarized here from Kisari Mohan Ganguli's translation (1883–96), begins with a detailed description of Dushyanta's hunting expedition, the force that accompanies him, and how, entering a forest, the king kills thousands of animals. He then enters a second forest with his men and, finally, after crossing a desert, exhausted by hunger and thirst, he reaches a third forest. This, unlike the others, is filled with flowering trees and the calls of birds. The River Malini flows close by, and upon its banks the king sees a hermitage, calm and serene, where smoke from holy fires rises into the sky and deer graze without fear upon green grass.

The king leaves his followers outside and enters the hermitage alone, where he is welcomed not by the sage as he had expected, but by the sage's beautiful and sweet-spoken daughter, Shakuntala. She explains that her father, the sage Kanva, has gone to gather some fruit but will be back soon. The king is aware that Kanva had taken a vow of celibacy, but Shakuntala willingly explains the circumstances of her birth. Menaka's seduction of Vishvamitra upon Indra's command is then given in some detail; though Shakuntala's birth by the River Malini and Menaka's abandonment of the newborn child is related quickly. In this version, the abandoned infant is protected by a flock of vultures, so that no wild animal could come near her. Kanva sees the baby surrounded by the raptors near the river and brings her to the hermitage, where, as in Kalidasa's play, she grows up as his daughter.

The king, now certain of her parentage and overcome with desire, asks her to marry him by the gandharva rite.

Shakuntala asks him to wait till her father returns after gathering fruit. But the king is impatient and persuades her to yield. She agrees on the condition that the son she bears him shall become his heir. Dushyanta agrees; after making love to her, and promising to send for her soon, he goes away. Kanva returns as soon as the king leaves. Shakuntala is too ashamed to tell him of her encounter with the king, but because of his ascetic powers, Kanva knows what has taken place in his absence. He gives his approval and blesses her, saying that her son will be a great king and invincible in battle.

In due course, the child is born; he is brought up in the hermitage as a king's son should be. He is named Sarvadamana, 'subduer of all'. When the boy turns six, Kanva deems that the time has come for him to be appointed heir apparent. He therefore sends Shakuntala and her son, escorted by his disciples, to the king in Hastinapura. The disciples introduce her to the king and return.

Shakuntala presents their son to Dushyanta, and reminding the king of his promise, asks that the child be made his heir. The king remembers his gandharva marriage with Shakuntala, but pretends that he has no recollection of any such encounter and dismisses her curtly. Shakuntala, hurt and indignant, protests that she is telling him the truth. Dushyanta cruelly calls her a liar and a wanton, of low birth, conceived in lust by the equally disreputable Menaka. He declares he does not recognize her and bids her leave. Shakuntala spiritedly defends herself and her mother, condemns him for a liar, points out that a father who abandons his child can never find favour with the gods, and leaves with her son.

As soon as Shakuntala leaves, a voice from the sky informs Dushyanta that she had spoken the truth, that her child was indeed his son, and that forsaking the child would bring down great misfortune upon the king. Dushyanta is delighted to hear this and declares that though he had known the child was his, he could not accept him on Shakuntala's word alone for the people would have questioned the child's legitimacy. Since the heavens themselves have declared the child to be his son, the king now accepts him with joy and makes him his heir. He also pacifies Shakuntala, forgives her angry words, and receives her as his wife. He renames the child 'Bharata', and in time the young prince becomes the greatest of all kings to ever rule this earth.

Kalidasa turns this prosaic, practical, and somewhat cynical tale into a poignant love story. In the *Mahabharata* version of the story, the king does not lose his memory, there is no curse to explain or excuse his behaviour, and he justifies his rejection of Shakuntala purely on social and political grounds; if the child's legitimacy is questioned, he cannot make the child his heir. Also, as king, his authority would be undermined if he was believed to have been cuckolded. Durvasa's curse, which absolves the king from any blame, is Kalidasa's innovation. Not only is Kalidasa's play one of the greatest dramas ever written, but the tale it tells has become over time the popular and generally accepted version of Shakuntala's story.

Commentaries

Several Sanskrit commentaries on *Abhijnanashakuntalam* are available to us. Perhaps the most popular of the old commentaries is Raghavabhatta's *Arthadyotanika*, written sometime during the last quarter of the fifteenth century CE.

Adaptations and Translations

Abhijnanashakuntalam was first translated into English in 1789 by Sir William Jones, founder of the Asiatic Society of Bengal. Jones, struggling to understand the nature of Sanskrit drama, was introduced to the play by the pandit Radhakanta Tarkavagisa. As related by Gillian Evison, in her essay 'The Sanskrit Manuscript of Sir William Jones', Jones acquired a copy of the play, and after a partial literal interlinear translation in Latin (preserved in the Bodleian Library in Oxford) and a literal translation in English, prepared a final English translation, free of 'foreign' idiom but faithful to Kalidasa's original. This final translation, called *Sacontalá* or *The Fatal Ring: An Indian Drama by Calidas* was published by Joseph Cooper in Calcutta in 1789. (A copy of this is also held at the Bodleian.)

Jones's translation was met with great acclaim in Europe. It was so popular that it was reprinted three times (London 1790 and 1792, and Edinburgh 1796) over the next seven years. His version was also translated into German by George Forster in 1791 and into French by A. Bruguière in 1803. The German poet Goethe was so taken with the play that he copied the convention of the sutradhara in the Prelude to his most celebrated work, *Faust*.

As a result of Jones's translation, Kalidasa was hailed as the finest dramatist of ancient India, and his *Abhijnanashakuntalam* as the finest literary work from any period. The play was translated, and its translations re-translated several times into English and other European languages such as Dutch, Swedish, Danish, and Italian.

In 1853, the British scholar Monier Monier-Williams, published the Sanskrit text of the play, and in 1855, his English translation, titled *Śakoontalá or The Lost Ring*.

More than any other work of Sanskrit literature, *Abhijnanashakuntalam* has caught the artistic imagination and inspired creative adaptations across the world – in ballet, opera, film, and art. In 1858, the first ballet version of the play was performed in Paris; the libretto was by the French poet Théophile Gautier and the music by the French composer Ernest Reyer. Subsequently, other ballet versions were composed and performed. In 1884, the Austrian composer Felix Weingartner composed *Sakuntala*, an opera based on Kalidasa's play.

In India, the play has permeated the cultural psyche at every level. It inspired one of Raja Ravi Varma's most celebrated paintings, of Shakuntala lingering for a last look at Dushyanta after their first meeting. It has also been adapted for film and television several times. The story of the 1985 film, *Ram, Teri Ganga Maili*, directed by celebrated actor and producer Raj Kapoor, bears an uncanny resemblance to that of Kalidasa's play. The film was a runaway success at the box-office. South Asia scholar and former professor of Hindi and Modern Indian Studies, Philip Lutgendorf, discusses the parallels in his 'note' on the film in 'Philip's Fil-ums: Notes on Popular Indian Cinema', his website on Hindi cinema.

The play has been translated several times into many Indian languages. These include Assamese, Bengali, Gujarati, Hindi, Kannada, Maithili, Malayalam, Marathi, Odia, Punjabi, Sindhi, Tamil, Telugu, and Urdu. A Farsi translation and at least one Chinese language translation (by scholar and

Indologist Ji Xianlin) also exist. Recent English translations include Barbara Stoler Miller's *Sakuntala and the Ring of Recollection* (*The Plays of Kalidasa*, UNESCO's Theater of Memory Project, 1984) and Chandra Rajan's *The Recognition of Sakuntala* (2002).

A Glimpse into 'Abhijnanashakuntalam'

Selected Excerpts from Act 4

Shakuntala's farewell as she prepares to leave Kanva's forest hermitage for Dushyanta's palace in the city.

KANVA.

Shakuntala must go to-day;
I miss her now at heart;
I dare not speak a loving word
Or choking tears will start.
My eyes are dim with anxious thought;
Love strikes me to the life:
And yet I strove for pious peace—
I have no child, no wife.
What must a father feel, when come
The pangs of parting from his child at home?

(He walks about.)

ANASUYA AND PRIYAMVADA.

There, Shakuntala, we have arranged your ornaments. Now put on this beautiful silk dress.

(Shakuntala rises and does so.)

GAUTAMI.
My child, here is your father. The eyes with which he seems to embrace you are overflowing with tears of joy. You must greet him properly.

(Shakuntala makes a shamefaced reverence.)

KANVA.

My child,
Like Sharmishtha, Yayati's wife,
Win favour measured by your worth;
And may you bear a kingly son
Like Puru, who shall rule the earth.

GAUTAMI.
My child, this is not a prayer, but a benediction.

KANVA.
My daughter, walk from left to right about the fires in which the offering has just been thrown.

(All walk about.)

The holy fires around the altar kindle,
And at their margins sacred grass is piled;
Beneath their sacrificial odours dwindle
Misfortunes. May the fires protect you, child!

(Shakuntala walks about them from left to right.)

KANVA.
Now you may start, my daughter. *(He glances about.)* Where are Sharngarava and Sharadvata?

(Enter the two pupils.)

THE TWO PUPILS.
We are here, Father.

KANVA.
Sharngarava, my son, lead the way for your sister.

SHARNGARAVA.
Follow me.

(They all walk about.)

KANVA.
O trees of the pious grove, in which the fairies dwell,
She would not drink till she had wet
Your roots, a sister's duty,
Nor pluck your flowers; she loves you yet
Far more than selfish beauty.
'Twas festival in her pure life
When budding blossoms showed;
And now she leaves you as a wife—
Oh, speed her on her road!

SHARNGARAVA *(listening to the song of the koel-birds)*.
Father,
The trees are answering your prayer
In cooing cuckoo-song,

Bidding Shakuntala farewell,
Their sister for so long.

INVISIBLE BEINGS.

May lily-dotted lakes delight your eye;
May shade-trees bid the heat of noonday cease;
May soft winds blow the lotus-pollen nigh;
May all your path be pleasantness and peace.

(All listen in astonishment.)

GAUTAMI.

My child, the fairies of the pious grove bid you farewell. For they love the household. Pay reverence to the holy ones.

(Shakuntala does so.)

SHAKUNTALA (*aside to Priyamvada*).

Priyamvada, I long to see my husband, and yet my feet will hardly move. It is hard, hard to leave the hermitage.

PRIYAMVADA.

You are not the only one to feel sad at this farewell. See how the whole grove feels at parting from you.

The grass drops from the feeding doe;
The peahen stops her dance;
Pale, trembling leaves are falling slow,
The tears of clinging plants.

***

Shakuntala bids goodbye to the fawn she has looked after since its birth.

SHAKUNTALA (*stumbling*).
Oh, oh! Who is it that keeps pulling at my dress, as if to hinder me? *(She turns round to see.)*

KANVA.
It is the fawn whose lip, when torn
By kusha-grass, you soothed with oil;
The fawn who gladly nibbled corn
Held in your hand; with loving toil
You have adopted him, and he
Would never leave you willingly.

SHAKUNTALA.
My dear, why should you follow me when I am going away from home? Your mother died when you were born and I brought you up. Now I am leaving you, and Father Kanva will take care of you. Go back, dear! Go back! *(She walks away, weeping.)*

KANVA.
Do not weep, my child. Be brave. Look at the path before you.
Be brave, and check the rising tears
That dim your lovely eyes;
Your feet are stumbling on the path
That so uneven lies.

An Excerpt from Act 6

Dushyanta has recovered his memory and is pining for Shakuntala. He calls for her portrait, which he himself has painted. The apsara Mishrakeshi eavesdrops on his conversation with his vidushaka, Madhavya.

KING.
O my darling, my heart burns with repentance because I abandoned you without reason. Take pity on me. Let me see you again.

(Enter Chaturika with the half-finished portrait of Shakuntala.)

CHATURIKA.
Your Majesty, here is the picture of our lady. *(She produces the painting.)*

KING *(gazing at it)*.

It is a beautiful picture. See!
A graceful arch of brows above great eyes;
Lips bathed in darting, smiling light that flies
Reflected from white teeth; a mouth as red
As red karkandhu-fruit; love's brightness shed
O'er all her face in bursts of liquid charm—
The picture speaks, with living beauty warm.

VIDUSHAKA *(looking at it)*.
The sketch is full of sweet meaning. My eyes seem to stumble over its uneven surface. What more can I say? I expect to see it come to life, and I feel like speaking to it.

MISHRAKESHI.
The king is a clever painter. I seem to see the dear girl before me.

KING.
My friend,

What in the picture is not fair,
Is badly done;

Yet something of her beauty there,
I feel, is won.

MISHRAKESHI.
This is natural, when love is increased by remorse.

KING (*sighing*).
I treated her with scorn and loathing ever;
Now o'er her pictured charms my heart will burst:
A traveller I, who scorned the mighty river,
And seeks in the mirage to quench his thirst.

– from *Kalidasa: Translations of Shakuntala and Other Works* by Arthur W. Ryder

MAHAKAVYA
or epic poetry

'Raghuvamsham' and 'Kumarasambhavam'

The mahakavya or 'great poem' is a long narrative poem that relates the deeds of gods, demigods, and legendary heroes of noble descent. It is similar to the western literary form known as the epic. Like most Sanskrit poetry it is highly stylized, and a poem, to be classified as a mahakavya, must conform to strict and elaborate rules that dictate structure, form, and content. For example, a mahakavya must consist of at least eight sargas or cantos, each in a single metre appropriate to its theme or subject matter; the hero must be brave and noble-minded; the poem must contain descriptions of mountains, forests, and cities; the dominant mood must be romantic, heroic, or conducive to tranquillity...and so on. Traditionally, a mahakavya is not concerned with the lives of ordinary men and women.

The form, derived from and influenced by the far more ancient *Ramayana* and *Mahabharata*, reached its highest expression between the fourth and eighth centuries CE. The great mahakavyas composed during this period include Kalidasa's *Raghuvamsham* and *Kumarasambhavam*.

Kalidasa's epics are immense in scope and imagination, the poetry powerful, evocative, even transcendental in parts.

Raghuvamsham, an account of the dynasty of Raghu, is set in a distant and legendary past, and located for the most part on earth. The second epic, *Kumarasambhavam*, is the story of the marriage of Shiva with Parvati. It is set in a primal age, almost at the beginning of creation, and located in the mythical world of gods and demons. Both epics are often described as 'unfinished'. We will see later why that is so.

Only a handful of the ancient mahakavyas are still available to us today. In addition to Kalidasa's two poems, the most important of these are *Janakiharana* by Kumaradasa (sixth century CE), *Kiratarjuniya* by Bharavi (sixth century CE), *Bhattikavya* by Bhatti (sixth or seventh century CE), and *Shishupalavadha* by Magha (seventh century CE); to this list of great mahakavyas is also added *Naishadhacharita*, composed somewhat later in 1174 CE by the philosopher–poet Shriharsha.

The ancient mahakavyas were composed under the patronage of kings and princes; they are therefore also called 'court epics'.

'Raghuvamsham' or The Lineage of Raghu

Raghuvamsham is a majestic and sweeping epic that describes the rise, expansion, and inevitable fall of a legendary line of kings divinely descended from the Sun. It is Kalidasa's most celebrated work in India, and has been extensively studied and commented upon through the centuries. It is also his longest work. The poem begins with Dilipa, a virtuous and capable monarch. Dilipa is succeeded by his son, the hero Raghu, who gives his name to the dynasty and to Kalidasa's epic. But the most important figure in the *Raghuvamsham* is Rama, the greatest king of the Raghu line. Rama is also the hero of Valmiki's *Ramayana*, and Kalidasa summarizes Valmiki's epic within his own. Kalidasa's great poem magnificently traverses legend and story as it explores the traditional ideal of kingship and the attributes of a perfect king.

Structure

The epic, in the form available to us today, consists of 1,557 stanzas arranged in 19 cantos.

Kalidasa uses 21 poetic metres across the 19 cantos of the poem.

Summary

The kings of the solar dynasty rule from Ayodhya, the capital of their kingdom, Uttara Kosala. In this line there are four great kings – Dilipa, Raghu, Aja, and Dasharatha. Dasharatha is followed by his son Rama, who is the incarnation of Vishnu on earth and the greatest of the solar kings. Rama is followed by 24 kings, the last of whom is Agnivarna, who dies leaving no heir.

The stories of Dasharatha and Rama are told in Cantos 9–15. Here, Kalidasa closely follows the *Ramayana*, but assuming that his audience is familiar with Valmiki's epic, often relates its main events in brief summary, sometimes in a line or two, and is selective about what he chooses to describe in detail. For instance, he condenses five of the seven books of the *Ramayana* – which is all that takes place from Rama's exile to the death of Ravana and Sita's eventual rescue – in a single section (Canto 12), describing only the final battle between Rama and Ravana at any length. However, he devotes all of Canto 13 to Rama's return to Ayodhya with Sita, describing their journey back in splendid and poetic detail. He also spends two cantos, 14 and 15, on Rama's renunciation of Sita, her eventual return into the earth, and Rama's death, a story he tells with empathy for Sita and not without understanding for Rama. Significantly, Kalidasa places Rama's birth at the beginning of Canto 10, the midpoint of the epic – this is appropriate given Rama's importance as Vishnu incarnate and the most glorious of the Raghu kings.

Canto 1

The epic opens with an invocation to Parvati and Shiva. After paying homage to the divine couple, the poet praises the illustrious solar dynasty. Considering his own intellect to be unequal to a description of this glorious dynasty, but attracted by the great virtues of the solar kings, he nevertheless decides to undertake this tremendous task, following the path laid out by older poets as his guide.

The first of the kings was Manu Vaivasvata; wise and virtuous, he was the son of the Sun. In direct descent from him comes Dilipa, a monarch tall and strong, like valour personified. His mind is as great as his body, his learning as expansive as his mind. He is a just king, learned, virtuous, and wise, and his only concern is the welfare of his subjects. His consort is Sudakshina, a princess from the royal line of Magadha, and though he has an entire harem at his disposal, he is solely devoted to her. But King Dilipa and his queen have no children.

So, one day, handing over the affairs of state to his ministers, Dilipa sets off with Sudakshina to the hermitage of the sage Vasishtha, their spiritual guide and guru. The sage, upon hearing their problem, explains that the king, unknown to him, is under a curse pronounced by the celestial cow Surabhi for once failing to pay her homage. In order to break the curse, the king must appease Surabhi's daughter Nandini, who happens to be Vasishtha's own cow. If pleased, Nandini could grant the king's wish for a son. The sage explains how to serve the cow, and the royal couple agree.

Canto 2

King Dilipa and Sudakshina serve the cow faithfully, exactly as the sage had instructed. Every morning the king follows the cow to the forest, where she grazes all day, and every evening, he returns with her to the hermitage. In this way, 21 days go by.

On the twenty-second day, the cow, instead of heading to her usual pasture, enters a mountain cave overgrown with fresh grass. The king, believing the cow to be safe, becomes engrossed in admiring the beauty of the mountain – till he suddenly hears a cry of distress. He turns to see that the cow has been attacked and seized by a lion. As the king reaches for an arrow, he finds he cannot move his arm.

The lion now speaks to him in a human voice. He explains that he is a servant of Shiva, who has set him there to guard a particular tree dear to Parvati against the depredations of wild elephants. Since he is not allowed to leave his post even for food, Shiva has given him permission to eat whatever animal comes within his reach, and so the cow is his to eat by right. The king is in a fix – he is unable to shoot the lion, but he cannot let the lion eat the cow. The only way out is to offer himself to the lion. The king does so, and after a long conversation, he succeeds in persuading the lion to accept him in place of the cow.

As soon as the lion agrees, the king finds he can move his arm again; he drops his weapons and braces himself for the lion's attack. But the lion vanishes and flowers rain down upon him from heaven – the lion was an illusion set up by the cow as a test. The cow, pleased with the king's actions, grants him and his queen the boon they had come seeking.

Canto 3

Dilipa and Sudakshina return to their capital city amid much rejoicing. Soon the queen becomes pregnant and, in time, gives birth to a son. The king is overjoyed; he names the young prince Raghu. The beloved child is educated in all the arts of kingship, and grows up into a tall and handsome man whose form surpasses even that of his father. He is then married, and appointed heir apparent.

Dilipa, his son by his side, becomes even more powerful. He entrusts Raghu with the sacred charge of guarding the sacrificial horse and performs, unhindered, ninety-nine ashvamedhas. He now decides to perform a hundredth sacrifice to equal Indra, king of the gods. But Indra does not allow this challenge to his power, and, making himself invisible, steals the sacrificial horse, guarded though it was by Raghu and his archers. Raghu is bewildered at the disappearance of the horse. Just then the cow Nandini appears and gives him the ability to see the invisible.

Raghu sees the god making off with the horse, and realizes it is Indra. He boldly asks Indra to return the horse. Indra, astonished at the young man's boldness and audacity, refuses – to him alone belongs the distinction of performing a hundred horse-sacrifices and he cannot allow another to take it away from him. Raghu, as the horse's guardian, challenges him to combat, and aims his arrows at him. This infuriates Indra, and a fierce battle now commences between the two. Indra ultimately strikes him with his thunderbolt. Raghu falls to the ground, but stands up again almost immediately, ready to continue to fight.

Indra, impressed by the young man's endurance and courage, offers him any gift he wants, except the horse. Raghu asks that Indra bestow upon his father the entire fruit of the sacrifice that would have accrued had it been completed, and requests he tell the king himself of what has occurred between them. Indra agrees and directs his charioteer to proceed at once to Dilipa's palace. Raghu, downcast at his failure, follows. He is met by his father, who has already heard the whole story; he welcomes his son, who now bears the mark of Indra's thunderbolt, with joy.

Shortly after, Dilipa yields his throne to Raghu and retires with Sudakshina to the forest, there to spend his old age free from worldly concerns.

Canto 4

Raghu's glory as king exceeds even that of his father. The season of rains ends and as autumn comes, making rivers fordable and drying muddy paths and tracks, Raghu embarks on a campaign of world conquest (digvijaya). After making his own kingdom secure, he sets off at the head of a massive army. He marches east, south, west, and north, bringing the entire Indian subcontinent under his sway. He also conquers the Parasikas, the ancient Persians, while the princes of Kamboja, afraid of his might, acknowledge him as their overlord.

Raghu's influence now stretches from the Brahmaputra and the delta of the Ganga in the east, to the Indus, Afghanistan, Baluchistan, and beyond in the west, from the

Himalayan mountains in the north to the Kaveri and Kerala in the south. Raghu is a formidable warrior who crushes every foe he faces and brings the whole world under his sway. But he is magnanimous in victory, a righteous king who treats his defeated enemies courteously.

The account of Raghu's campaign is one of the most celebrated passages in the *Raghuvamsham*. Kalidasa describes Raghu's route across the subcontinent in detail (with names and locations of mountain ranges, rivers, forests, countries, and kingdoms) with such accuracy that it may be traced easily on a modern map. He describes, too, the battles – the armies and military tactics of his foes, the armour and attire of enemy soldiers, Raghu's many victories, and the gifts he receives as tribute. The battle against Kalinga is especially fierce. Raghu, triumphant, takes the ruler of Kalinga prisoner but later, having proven his superiority, reinstates him as king.

We hear of the boats the Bangas of the Ganga delta use to fight Raghu, of the enormous elephants of the mighty Kalinga army, the helmets and bearded faces of the Persians, and the iron arrows of mountain-dwelling tribes. We know that the Bangas fill Raghu's granary with grain, while the Pandya princes give him fine pearls. Kalidasa describes the eastern coast of peninsular India, lined with betel-nut palms, and palm toddy that his soldiers drink from cups made from folded betel leaves. He tells us of the pepper fields in the south, where parrots flit through forests, the air smells of cardamom, and serpents coil in sandalwood trees; and of the western coast along which runs the Sahyadri range and where the river breeze, rustling through the fronds of date palm trees, is scented with the fragrance of screw pine. Kalidasa captures the noise and dust of battle as easily as he does the natural beauty of the lands and the colourful diversity of the people Raghu encounters.

Raghu returns in triumph to his own kingdom of Kosala with the kings he had defeated and deprived of their kingdoms. He then performs the vishvajit (literally 'world victory') sacrifice, during which he gives away all he has, for the only purpose of acquisition is distribution for the good of others. After the completion of the sacrifice, he permits the conquered kings to return home, soothing their feelings of defeat and humiliation with friendship and rich gifts.

Canto 5

After the vishvajit sacrifice, an ascetic called Kautsa comes to see Raghu. The ascetic, having completed his education, has come to ask the king for money to pay his teacher's fee. Raghu, who has given away all his possessions during the sacrifice, nevertheless welcomes him most hospitably. He has no gold, so he takes him water in an earthen cup. The ascetic, seeing the cup of clay, realizes Raghu has given away all his wealth. He blesses the king and prepares to leave, saying that he will seek elsewhere the fee he owes his guru. But Raghu cannot let this happen. For him, it is unthinkable that a scholar asks him for help to pay his guru's fee and, failing to receive it from him, has to turn to another for the money.

Raghu stops the ascetic from leaving and asks how much he owes his teacher. The ascetic explains that his teacher had initially asked no fee, but when urged to accept at least some amount, had become annoyed and then asked for the exorbitant sum of 14 crores, which was well beyond his means. Raghu invites the ascetic to stay a few days in his temple while he arranges to get the money.

Raghu decides to take the required sum from Kubera, the god of wealth, by force. But just as he is about to set forth, a shower of gold falls into his treasury – Kubera has understood Raghu's intention and, afraid of being attacked, fills his treasury with wealth. Raghu gives the entire pile of shining gold to Kautsa. Both men are praised by the people of Ayodhya, the king for giving more than he had been asked for, the ascetic for not taking more than he needed for his guru's fee. Kautsa then bids farewell to the king with the blessing that a son would soon be born to Raghu.

In time, Raghu's queen gives birth to a boy as handsome and noble as his father. This child is named Aja. When Aja is old enough to be married, a message arrives from King Bhoja of Vidarbha inviting the prince to the king's sister Indumati's svayamvara, the ceremony at which she would choose her husband. Raghu, thinking this a worthy alliance, sends his son to Vidarbha, accompanied by an army.

After travelling some distance, Aja and his men make camp by the banks of the River Narmada. Suddenly, a wild elephant emerges from the river. The elephant is in rut, and the tame elephants in Aja's army are frightened by it and run away from their mahouts. The entire camp is thrown into turmoil. Aja shoots an arrow at the wild elephant's head, seeking not to kill but merely to stop him.

As soon Aja's arrow pierces the elephant's forehead, the giant beast sheds his elephant shape and takes on the radiant form of a celestial being. The heavenly being explains that he is Priyamvada, the son of Priyadarshana, king of the gandharvas. He had been turned into a wild elephant due to a curse, which has now been broken by Aja's arrow. In gratitude, he gives Aja a magical, sleep-inducing weapon called Sammohana. The prince accepts the gandharva's gift; Priyamvada returns to his heavenly abode, while the prince continues on his journey to Vidarbha.

Upon reaching King Bhoja's city, Aja is welcomed with great ceremony by the king himself. He rests for the night and, next morning, makes his way to the svayamvara ceremony.

Canto 6

Aja takes his seat in the assembly hall amid the other mighty kings and princes who have come in the hope of being chosen by Indumati. Though each king there is a hero in his own right, Aja outshines them all. As the princess arrives in a palanquin carried by four men and surrounded by members of her family, all eyes turn towards her. Each great prince strives to look his best – like any boy trying to impress a girl. One is bashful, another continues to talk casually to a friend, one adjusts a sash, another a jewel-studded crown.

Then Sunanda, doorkeeper of the women's apartments, leads the princess to each of the kings assembled there, introduces him, and describes his attributes to her. Among the princess's suitors are the rulers of Magadha, Anga, Avanti, Anupa, Shurasena, Kalinga, and the Pandya king of Uraga city. But Indumati passes them all by. Sunanda then leads her to Aja, and, without a moment's hesitation, the princess chooses him as her husband. The people of Vidarbha are overjoyed, but the other kings, their hopes destroyed, are silent.

Canto 7

King Bhoja then returns to his capital with Indumati and Aja. The rejected suitors return angrily to their camps. As Aja and Indumati pass through the city, women rush to the windows to catch a glimpse of the bridegroom. They cannot praise the handsome couple enough.

After the wedding ceremony, which takes place in the royal palace, Aja and Indumati leave for Ayodhya with their attendants. Meanwhile, the other kings, furious at their rejection, decide to forcibly take the princess for themselves. They ambush the royal party on the way to Ayodhya and surround Aja. The prince assigns a trusted officer and numerous soldiers to protect the princess, and, with his remaining soldiers, fights the jealous kings and their armies. A fierce battle now ensues. Aja finally uses the Sammohana, the weapon the gandharva had given him, and all the other kings and their soldiers fall asleep.

Aja returns to Ayodhya with Indumati. They are welcomed by Raghu, who has already received the news of their wedding. Raghu entrusts the kingdom to Aja, for he now wishes to retire from the worldly duties of a king.

Canto 8

Aja is crowned king. He is equal in glory to his father and as virtuous. He is especially beloved of the people for his youth, and his kindness and innate goodness. Raghu, seeing his son firmly established on the throne, wishes to leave for the forest. But Aja tearfully begs him not to abandon him, so Raghu retires to a hermitage outside the city. Aja grows in splendour as a wise and just king. In time, Raghu dies and Aja gives him a suitable funeral.

Soon, Indumati gives birth to a son who is named Dasharatha. As is well-known, Dasharatha becomes the father of Rama. King Aja now lacks for nothing; he continues to rule his kingdom with compassion, wisdom, and justice.

One day, Aja and Indumati are in their pleasure garden when a wreath of flowers falls from the sky upon the queen who instantly collapses and dies. Aja is inconsolable. His lament, as he holds her body in his arms, is long and heartbreaking. His guru explains that Indumati was actually the apsara Harini, bound by a sage's curse to be born a human till she sees celestial flowers. The curse had been broken by the heavenly wreath falling upon her.

The guru advises the king not to grieve, for death is the inevitable outcome of birth. Despite his guru's wise words, Aja is unable to accept his wife's death. He somehow lives another eight years till his son, the prince, is grown. Then, entrusting his kingdom and the people to his care, Aja departs this life. He is united again in heaven with his beloved Indumati.

Canto 9

Dasharatha rules the kingdom of Uttara Kosala as ably as his father and grandfather. He is learned, wise, and a skilled warrior whom even Indra asks for help on occasion. In time, he marries three princesses, the daughters of the kings of Kosala, Magadha, and Kaikeya.

One beautiful spring day, Dasharatha decides to go hunting. He leaves for the forest with a group of close friends. He meets with so much success that he forgets his duties as king and extends the hunt. One morning, he rides off alone after a deer. He reaches the banks of the River Tamasa where he hears the gurgling sound of a pot being filled with water. Mistaking it for an elephant's grunt, he shoots an arrow in that direction, aiming by sound alone. He hears a cry and finds, hidden in the reeds by the river's bank, a young ascetic boy with a water pot; the boy has been wounded by his arrow. The horrified king realizes his mistake. He carries the injured

boy to his aged parents, who are both blind, and tells them how he unwittingly hurt their son.

The ascetic couple make the king pull his arrow out of their son's chest, but the boy's wound is fatal and he dies. The father, in his grief, curses the king, that he too will die lamenting in his old age for his son. The king, who had no son yet, accepts the curse as a backhanded blessing, for at least it meant he would have a son before he died. The old couple burn themselves on their son's funeral pyre. Dasharatha returns to his capital, shaken by the incident and carrying the curse within him.

Canto 10

Many, many years pass. Dasharatha rules his kingdom in splendour, his glory equal to Indra's. But he still has no son. The royal priests are equally anxious for the birth of an heir; at last, they begin, on the king's behalf, the performance of a special fire-sacrifice that would lead to the birth of a son.

At about this time, the gods, overwhelmed by Ravana, the powerful king of the rakshasas, go to Vishnu for help. Vishnu, just awakened from his yogic sleep, is seated upon the shining coils of the many-hooded serpent Shesha, his foot in the lap of his consort Lakshmi, his white garments as bright as a day in autumn; upon his chest glows the Kaustubha jewel and his long arms are adorned with gems. With him are his weapons and his mount, the celestial eagle, Garuda. Vishnu is aware of the scourge that is Ravana. He explains to the gods that Brahma, pleased by Ravana's penance, had granted him the boon he wanted – which was that he may not be killed by the gods. But, despising the human race, Ravana had not asked for immunity from death at the hands of a man. Vishnu reassures the gods and promises that he will take birth as the son of Dasharatha, and in that mortal form, kill Ravana.

Now, as Dasharatha's priests complete the sacrifice for a royal heir, out of the fire there steps a being holding in both hands a golden bowl full of kheer (rice boiled with milk). The container is difficult to hold even for the divine being, for the kheer in it is infused with the essence of Vishnu. The king accepts the bowl of kheer and gives half the contents to Kaushalya, his eldest queen, and half to Kaikeyi, whom he loved most of all. Each of the two queens, knowing the king did not wish to leave out Sumitra, his third queen, gives half her portion to her.

The three queens become pregnant and in time give birth to sons. Kaushalya gives birth to Rama, the eldest; Kaikeyi gives birth to Bharata, and Sumitra to the twins Lakshmana and Shatrughna. The four brothers are all partial incarnations of Vishnu. Their birth is celebrated with music and festivities. The four brothers grow up in harmony with each other – there is no rivalry among them, though Lakshmana is inseparable from Rama, and Shatrughna from Bharata. They add to Dasharatha's glory and are his pride and joy.

Canto 11

While the princes are still boys, the great sage Kaushika (Vishvamitra) comes to Dasharatha's court. He requests that the king send Rama with him to guard his sacrificial rites, which were being disturbed by rakshasas. Dasharatha, who never turns away a supplicant, agrees and, despite their tender years, sends Rama and Lakshmana with the sage. The boys take leave of their tearful father and their mothers, and set off with the sage for his forest hermitage.

On the way, they encounter the demon Tadaka; though Rama is reluctant to kill a woman, he does not hesitate when she attacks them, and kills her with an arrow to the heart. In praise of this feat, the sage gives Rama a mantra to destroy demons. They also pass by the hermitage of Vamana, an earlier incarnation of Vishnu. Upon reaching Kaushika's hermitage, the boys stand guard as the ascetics begin their sacrificial rites. The demons appear in the sky overhead and, led by Tadaka's son and the rakshasa Subahu, disrupt the rite by spattering the altar with blood. Rama kills the two leaders and the demons flee.

Kaushika now visits the city of Mithila at the invitation of its king, Janaka, for the performance of a sacrifice. He takes along the two princes, who had heard about Shiva's great bow held by Janaka and were curious to see it. On the way they pass a beautiful hermitage where the wife of the sage Gautama had been turned into a rock for once being with Indra as his wife. The touch of Rama's feet restores her to her human form.

As Kaushika and the two princes approach Mithila, Janaka comes out to greet them. The sacrifice completed, Kaushika tells Janaka about Rama's desire to see the bow. Janaka had made it known that whoever succeeds in bending the great bow would receive his daughter Sita's hand in marriage. Not even the most powerful warrior had been able to bend the bow, and Janaka, looking at Rama's slender form, is troubled. But Rama picks up the bow and strings it effortlessly; he draws it with such strength that the great bow snaps with a sound like thunder.

Janaka keeps his word and gives Sita in marriage to Rama. He sends word to Dasharatha, who is delighted and hurries with his army to Mithila. The wedding ceremony of Rama and Sita takes place. Lakshmana is also married, to Sita's younger sister Urmila, and the twins Bharata and Shatrughna, to the two daughters of Janaka's brother Kushadhvaja.

As Dasharatha and the four princes with their brides set off for their own city of Ayodhya, they are stopped by the sage Parashurama. His father had been killed by the sons of the king of the Haihaiyas; in vengeance, Parashurama had vowed to rid the earth of all warriors. Angered now by Rama's exploit with Shiva's bow, he fixes his flaming eyes upon Rama and challenges him to string his, Parashurama's, bow.

Now Parashurama is actually Vishnu's previous incarnation on earth, and his bow is Vishnu's own. Rama, who is also Vishnu incarnate, therefore easily lifts and strings the bow. Parashurama recognizes him as Vishnu and leaves for heaven. Dasharatha and his sons and daughters-in-law now resume their journey and arrive safely in Ayodhya after a few days.

Canto 12

King Dasharatha has grown old and, knowing that his end is near, decides to set Rama upon the throne. The people of Ayodhya welcome this news with great joy. But Kaikeyi is not happy and invokes the two boons the king had once granted her – as her first boon she asks that Rama be exiled to the forest for 14 years, and as the second that her son Bharata be made king. Rama accepts the exile with equanimity and leaves for the Dandaka forest, accompanied by Sita and Lakshmana. The king, unable to bear this separation from Rama and recalling the blind ascetic's curse, dies of grief.

The people of Ayodhya send for Bharata, who is away visiting his uncle. Upon returning, Bharata turns away from his mother, refuses the throne, and goes with the army to

Chitrakuta, where Rama and Lakshmana now live. He tells Rama of their father's death and pleads with him to ascend the throne. But Rama refuses to go against his father's decree. Bharata finally leaves, taking a pair of Rama's sandals to place on the throne in his stead; he refuses to enter Ayodhya but lives in Nandigrama, a village on its outskirts, from where he rules the kingdom in Rama's name.

Rama lives peacefully in the forest with Sita and Lakshmana. Concerned that Chitrakuta's proximity to Ayodhya might tempt Bharata to return, Rama, Sita, and Lakshmana move southwards. As they move through the forest, they encounter a rakshasa called Viradha, who boldly carries off Sita; he is killed by the two brothers and his body consigned to flames.

Rama, Sita, and Lakshmana then take up residence in Panchavati. Here, Shurpanakha, Ravana's younger sister, attracted by Rama's handsome looks, comes to him in the form of a pretty young woman. He turns her away, admonishing her that he has a wife, and sends her to Lakshmana. But Lakshmana also refuses her advances, and she returns to Rama. Sita laughs at her predicament, which enrages Shurpanakha, who then reveals her true form. Lakshmana, realizing that she is a rakshasi, mutilates her face with his sword.

Howling with rage, Shurpanakha leaps into the sky and flies to the rakshasa Khara; she tells him and the other rakshasas of her humiliation at the hands of the two brothers. Khara attacks Rama with an enormous demon army. Instructing Lakshmana to look after Sita, Rama faces the rakshasas on his own and single-handedly kills them all. Shurpanakha alone remains alive; she now informs Ravana of all that has taken place.

Ravana is furious, and, with the help of another rakshasa who takes on the form of a deer, he tricks Rama and

Lakshmana and carries off Sita. A vulture, a lord among birds and grateful to Dasharatha for his friendship, tries to stop him but fails. As the two brothers search for Sita, they find the vulture, his wings cut off, and mortally wounded. The dying bird tells them of Sita's abduction by Ravana, and his own fruitless attempt to stop him. The brothers perform the bird's last rites. Rama then frees the demon Kabandha from a curse, and on his advice befriends Sugriva, a monkey-prince.

Rama kills Sugriva's brother and rival Bali, and installs Sugriva as king in his place. In return, Sugriva sends out his monkey troops to search for Sita. They find that she is being held a prisoner in Lanka. Maruti (Hanuman) then crosses the ocean and finds Sita, guarded by frightening rakshasis. After reassuring Sita and giving her Rama's ring, he allows himself to be captured; he then frees himself, setting the city of Lanka on fire. Maruti returns to Rama with Sita's ring. Rama now marches to Lanka with the entire monkey army. Ravana's brother, Vibhishana, joins Rama.

Rama then has a bridge built across the sea to Lanka. He crosses over with the monkey army. A series of fearsome battles take place between the monkeys and the rakshasas. At one point, Sita thinks Rama's head has been cut off and faints, but it turns out to be an illusion. At another point, Rama and Lakshmana are caught by Meghanada (Ravana's eldest son) in his serpent snares, but are freed by Garuda. Lakshmana is then seriously wounded, but revived by an herb brought by Maruti. Lakshmana kills Meghanada, while Rama kills Ravana's brother, Kumbhakarna.

Finally, Rama and Ravana face each other on the battlefield. Seeing Ravana in a chariot and Rama on foot, Indra sends Rama a chariot driven by his own charioteer Matali, as well as his own armour. Ravana is present in all his glory. Despite all his evil ways, he is a great warrior who has performed great deeds, and Rama considers him a worthy foe. A fierce duel now takes place between the two. Finally, Rama strikes Ravana with Brahma's divine weapon and slices off all of Ravana's ten heads as the gods watch in disbelief. Rama, having achieved his purpose, now puts away his weapons, and the gods shower him with flowers.

Rama welcomes Sita, her chastity proven by fire, and places Vibhishana on the throne of Lanka. Then, with Sita by his side, Rama mounts the flying chariot Pushpaka, and attended by Lakshmana, and Sugriva and Vibhishana with their armies, sets off for Ayodhya.

Canto 13

As they fly to Ayodhya, Rama lovingly points out various sights to Sita. He describes the ocean and tells her of the pearls that grow within it, the strange serpents and water creatures that inhabit its waves, and the rivers that flow into it, and reminds her of the ancient stories associated with it. As they reach the farther shore, he describes the palm and tamala trees that grow along the coastline, and the sandy beaches covered with shells.

Farther inland, he points out the places where he had searched for her. He tells her of the anklet he had found, cast off by her as Ravana had carried her through the skies, and his tears of grief at being parted from her. He shows her hermitages belonging to renowned ascetics, and points out Chitrakuta where they had spent many pleasant and loving moments together at the beginning of their forest exile. They fly over the sacred Ganga and the Yamuna, and the town where he had cast off his princely robes for a hermit's garb and bid farewell to Dasharatha's weeping charioteer who had accompanied them thus far from Ayodhya.

At last, they come to the River Sarayu, which flows through their kingdom of Uttara Kosala and nourishes the people of Ayodhya. Ahead, they see a cloud of dust – it is Bharata who has been told of their approach by Hanuman and who has come to welcome them with an army. He is on foot, clad in ascetic garments of tree bark, and preceded by their guru.

Rama brings the flying chariot to land. Rama and Bharata tearfully embrace each other, as do Bharata and Lakshmana. Rama introduces his friends and allies to his brother. Sugriva takes on human form and mounts an elephant, and Vibhishana and his men mount their chariots. Rama and his brothers climb aboard the flying chariot, where Bharata bows in reverence to Sita. Then, accompanied by the people who had come to greet them, they enter Ayodhya, where Shatrughna is waiting to greet them.

Canto 14

Together, Rama and Lakshmana meet their two mothers. The queens, wasted with grief, greet their children with tears of joy. Sita touches the feet of her mothers-in-law who welcome her with words of love. Rama is then crowned king and rides through Ayodhya in state, attended by his three brothers. Sita follows in a palanquin, and the women of Ayodhya gather at their windows to see her pass. Rama then enters the royal palace, where now only a portrait of his father remains. He then goes to see Kaikeyi, and eases her guilt and disgrace with gentle words. The sages who had come for his consecration, as well as his allies, Sugriva and Vibhishana, depart. Rama restores the flying chariot to Kubera, its rightful owner.

Rama now begins to rule as king with Sita ever present at his side. The memories of their forest exile no longer hurt and serve only to increase their present joy. He treats his mothers – the three queens – with equal respect and his younger brothers with love. He is a good king, devoted to his people who are, in turn, devoted to him.

A new joy now comes into Rama's life – his beloved Sita is pregnant. She expresses a wish to visit again the hermit groves along the Ganga that she had once known well. Rama, eager to please her, agrees. But, as he stands upon the palace roof, surveying the city of Ayodhya, he becomes curious to know how his subjects speak of him; his attendant, forced to answer, replies that they approve of all he does, except his acceptance of Sita after she had lived for so long in a rakshasa's house. Rama is shattered to hear this – he knows Sita is chaste, but he cannot allow such a rumour to circulate. He decides that the only way to salvage his reputation is to give up his innocent wife. He summons his younger brothers and tells them of his decision. His brothers are unwilling to support him, but equally, they cannot oppose him. Rama then orders Lakshmana, who has always done as he commanded, to take Sita to Valmiki's hermitage and leave her there.

Lakshmana reluctantly accepts Rama's command. Sita goes willingly with him to the forest, suspecting nothing, thinking only that Rama had fulfilled her wish to visit the hermit groves. Lakshmana escorts her to Valmiki's grove, and there, weeping inconsolably, tells her of Rama's cruel command. Sita faints in shock, but is revived by Lakshmana, who then shows her Valmiki's hermitage. He asks her to forgive him, forced as he was to follow Rama's order. Sita gives him her blessing, and asks him to let her mothers-in-law know that she carries Rama's seed within her. She also gives him a sorrowful but dignified message for her husband, blaming herself rather than Rama for her situation.

Lakshmana leaves, and once he is out of sight, Sita weeps and wails in fear and grief. Valmiki hears her crying, and comes to find her. Through the power of meditation, he knows all that has happened. He gives her shelter in his hermitage as a father would his daughter. She begins to live there, looked after by the women ascetics.

Lakshmana returns to Ayodhya and gives Rama her message. Rama is reduced to tears, for though he has banished Sita from his kingdom, he still holds her in his heart. Then, putting away his grief, he turns to affairs of state and proceeds to rule his kingdom. He does not marry again but keeps a golden image of Sita by his side.

Canto 15

Rama devotes himself fully to his duties as king. Ascetics living along the Yamuna now come to him, seeking his help against Lavana, a powerful rakshasa. Rama sends Shatrughna along with an army to deal with the demon. On the way, Shatrughna stops at Valmiki's hermitage, and that very night, Sita gives birth to twins. Shatrughna is delighted to hear the news, but leaves without revealing himself to Sita. He then proceeds to battle Lavana and kills him.

Feeling a worthy brother to Rama at last, he holds his head up high, and on the banks of the Yamuna builds the beautiful city of Mathura. In time, he has two sons, named Subahu and Bahushruta, to whom he eventually gives the cities of Mathura and Vidisha. Meanwhile, Sita's sons, who are named Kusha and Lava, are growing up in Valmiki's hermitage. The sage teaches them the Vedas and to sing his own poem *Ramayana* that recounts the deeds of their father. After some time, Shatrughna returns to Ayodhya, but, at Valmiki's request, says nothing to Rama about Kusha and Lava.

Rama continues to rule, maintaining peace in his kingdom and upholding the social order. He now decides to hold the ashvamedha or horse-sacrifice. Sages and ascetics come from the celestial realms and all quarters of the earth. Valmiki comes as well, bringing with him Kusha and Lava. Rama places Sita's golden image by his side and the sacrifice begins. Valmiki now urges the twins to sing his *Ramayana*. The two boys charm everyone, including Rama and his brothers, by their sweet voices and handsome looks.

All those who see the boys are amazed at how similar they look to Rama. Valmiki tells Rama that they are his sons by Sita, and pleads that he take Sita back. Rama replies that though he knows Sita is pure, she must convince the people of her chastity – only then would the rumours end and only then would he be able to take her back.

Accordingly, the sage brings Sita and her two sons before Rama and a gathering of his subjects. Sita then calls upon the Earth, her mother, to take her if she has been truly pure and faithful to her husband. At this, the goddess Earth rises out of the ground, and taking Sita in her arms, disappears into the earth. Rama, now wanting Sita back, is left fuming, but he can do nothing against destiny.

Rama bestows all the love he had for Sita upon their two sons. He puts his brothers and their sons in charge of various parts of the kingdom. Then, together with his brothers, he performs the last rites for their three mothers, the three widowed queens who had finally left the world to join their husband, Dasharatha.

Rama now realizes that his time on earth is coming to an end. Lakshmana is the first of the four brothers to die. After his death, Rama loses whatever interest he had left in the world. He gives Kusha the city of Kushavati, and Lava the city of Sharavati. Accompanied by Bharata and Shatrughna, and followed by his old friends and allies, he leaves Ayodhya. He enters the River Sarayu, and together with his brothers and all those devoted to him, ascends to heaven. His work on earth now complete, Vishnu resumes his own true form.

Canto 16

Kusha is now acknowledged as supreme among them by his brother and his six cousins, the sons of his three uncles. One night, as Kusha lies asleep, the guardian deity of Ayodhya comes to him in a dream. She is dressed in mourning like a widow, and beseeches him to return to Ayodhya and restore the now-deserted city to its former glory. Kusha agrees, and, handing over the governance of Kushavati to learned men, returns to Ayodhya, accompanied by his household and his army. Under his capable rule, Ayodhya soon regains its splendour.

One summer, while playing and swimming in the Sarayu with the women of his harem, his armlet, unnoticed by him, falls into the river. The armlet had been given to him by his father, and Kusha cannot bear to lose it. He orders the river to be searched, but his divers come up empty-handed and declare it has been taken by the serpent king Kumuda, who lived in that stretch of the river.

Kusha goes to the riverbank and arms his bow with a missile to kill the serpent king. As he prepares to shoot,

Kumuda rises out of the river with Kusha's ornament and holding a beautiful young girl by the hand. Kusha lowers his weapon, and Kumuda explains that the young woman with him is his sister Kumudavati, and that she had taken the armlet out of curiosity. He requests Kusha to marry his sister and Kusha agrees. The wedding takes place duly, uniting the Raghu dynasty with that of the serpent kings.

Canto 17

From Kumudavati is born Kusha's son Atithi. He is as radiant as his father, and endowed with every noble quality. He is educated in a manner appropriate to a Raghu king, and when he is older, he is married. Kusha then assists Indra against the rakshasa Durjaya; he kills the demon, but is also killed by him. Kumudavati follows her husband in death.

Atithi is then crowned king in a magnificent coronation ceremony. He is as glorious as Indra, strong, powerful, and endowed with good looks and wisdom. He is an able administrator, generous and just, and skilled in statecraft. He performs the ashvamedha and other kings willingly accept him as their overlord. The gods smoothen his way and make his rule easy and prosperous.

Canto 18

This canto lists, without too much detail, the various kings who succeed Atithi. The first is Atithi's son, Nishadha. The others, twenty in all, are Nala, Nabha, Pundarika, Kshemadhanva, Devanika, Ahinagu, Pariyatra, Shila, Unnabha, Vajranabha, Shankhana, Vyushitashva,

Vishvasaha, Hiranyanabha, Kausalya, Brahmishtha, Putra, Pushya, Dhruvasandhi, and Sudarshana.

Sudarshana is still a child, only six years old, when his father, Dhruvasandhi, is killed by a lion while hunting. He is nevertheless crowned king, a title and role he fulfils with dignity despite his tender years. He grows up into a handsome and able king, and is married to various princesses, each eager to be his wife.

Canto 19

Sudarshana, now grown old, gives the throne to his son Agnivarna, and retires to a life of penance in the forest. The new king rules well for a time, but being by nature lustful, hands over the governance of the kingdom to his ministers and devotes himself to the pleasures of the flesh. He is constantly surrounded by women, and his queens, angry and frustrated, organize love festivals in a vain attempt to gain his attention. His dissolute and dissipated lifestyle takes its toll, and he dies from an illness his doctors are unable to cure. He is cremated quickly and secretly by his minsters in the garden of his house. His grieving queen, pregnant with his child, is set on the throne. She rules her husband's realm on behalf of her unborn child, whose birth is eagerly anticipated by the people.

On this uncertain but hopeful note, the epic ends.

An Unfinished Epic?

Though regarded as a complete poem by the ancient Sanskrit commentators, its rather sudden end and the lack of a closing benedictory stanza has led modern scholars such as M.R. Kale to question whether it is indeed a finished piece of work. Kale points out that the *Vishnupurana* lists 37 more kings after Agnivarna. He also reminds us that in Sanskrit poetry, a happy or pleasing end was almost mandatory, and it is unlikely that Kalidasa would have chosen to end his epic with the death of a major character. He therefore asks whether the poet might not have written more cantos than have come down to us, and points to a 'persistent tradition' that says that the original poem consisted of 25 cantos.

Scholar and translator Chandra Rajan, in her introduction to Kalidasa's poems, terms the epic 'formally complete', but 'aesthetically unfinished'. The final stanza, in her words, is 'open-ended'. It offers hope – perhaps the pregnant queen will give birth to a son to carry on the Raghu line! Equally, though, it makes no promises except uncertainty – what if the queen fails to carry the child to term or gives birth to a daughter? If so, will she still continue to rule? If not, who will replace her? Is this, then, truly the end of the Raghu line? We do not know. The epic gives no answers, and in that sense, it may be called 'unfinished'.

Inspiration for 'Raghuvamsham'

The stories of the solar kings must have been well-known in Kalidasa's time, in folklore as well as through Puranic and other literature, in particular, Valmiki's great epic. Kalidasa was clearly well-acquainted with all these sources, picking and choosing from them as he pleased. He mentions Valmiki and his *Ramayana* with reverence and has used it as his primary source for the stories of Dasharatha and Rama. But the scope of Kalidasa's epic extends well beyond the *Ramayana*.

In the initial stanzas of his epic, he states, rather vaguely, that he has followed the words of 'ancient sages' and what has long been heard in writing his account of the virtues of the kings of the solar dynasty. He does not specify these ancient scholars. Perhaps they were the early authors of the Puranas, though given that the Puranas have been extensively and continuously revised through the centuries, it is difficult to say so with any confidence. In fact, it is likely that the Puranas were revised to incorporate Kalidasa's stories and used his works as source material rather than vice versa.

Commentaries

Raghuvamsham, for its subject matter as much as for its poetry, is Kalidasa's most admired work in India. Its popularity through the centuries can be gauged by the thousands of manuscripts available to us today. The epic also has the largest number of Sanskrit commentaries of all Kalidasa's works, and multiple manuscripts of more than 50 commentaries, from all parts of the country, also survive to the present day. The earliest of the commentaries known to us today is the tenth-century *Panjika* by the Kashmiri scholar Vallabhadeva; the best-known and most popular is the fourteenth-century *Sanjivani* by the Telugu critic and commentator Mallinatha Suri.

Adaptations and Translations

The epic has been translated more than once into major Indian languages, including Bengali, Gujarati, Hindi, Kannada, Maithili, Malayalam, Marathi, Odia, Tamil, and Telugu. A notable early translation is a sixteenth-century translation into Tamil by Arakesari, prince of Jaffna. Several English translations exist, the more recent among them A.N.D. Haksar's *Raghuvamsam: The Line of Raghu* (2016) and the Murty Classical Library's *The Lineage of the Raghus* (2023) edited and translated by Csaba Dezső, Dominic Goodall, and Harunaga Isaacson.

A Glimpse into 'Raghuvamsham'

From Canto 4

Raghu sets off on his campaign of world conquest.

His palace and the forts protected,
his armed force's rear secured,
he set forth with a sixfold army,
seeking world-wide victory. 26

Old city women sent him off
in a shower of rice grains,
like foam flecks on Vishnu raining
when breakers from the sea of milk
crash on the Mandara mountain. 27

He was like another Indra,
and he eastwards headed first,
his banners tossing in the wind,
as if to warn adversaries. 28

With elephants looking like dark clouds
and chariots raising clouds of dust,

he made the earth look like the sky
and the sky just as the earth. 29

The army moved to fourfold beats,
first of glory, then of tumult,
after that the dust, the chariots
and the rest just marched behind. 30

And, with his power he transformed
deserts into watered land,
brightened dark forests, made
fordable rivers that needed boats. 31

He led an enormous army,
Like Bhagiratha did the Ganga
When she from Shiva's locks cascaded. 32

From Canto 8

From Aja's lament at the sudden death of his beloved queen, Indumati, by a wreath of heavenly flowers falling on her from the sky.

'If flowers falling on the body
are able to take life away,
alas, what other means might fate
possess to strike another too? 44

Or is it that death destroys only
the tender with such methods soft?
Like the lily, which I know,
can be by a snowflake felled. 45

Indeed, if this wreath took her life
then, placed upon my heart, O why
does it not kill me? Or is it
that, at times, by will divine,
even nectar into poison turns,
or the other way around? 46

Or was it a quirk in my destiny
that fate designed a thunderbolt
by which this tree was not destroyed,
only the vine which clings to it?' 47

***

'But, my love, the wind does ruffle
your wavy hair, with flowers dressed,
bringing to my mind the thought
that you are coming back to me! 53

Darling, with your wake-up call,
be quick and dispel my grief,
light up the darkness of this cave
with a flaming torch tonight. 54

But this face, with hair dishevelled,
grieves me for it does not speak,
it is the lotus closed at night,
with a bee inside it, silent. 55

The night does meet the moon again,
so does the loving bird its mate:

this helps them bear their separation.
But you have gone for good, and so
How can this not burn me out?' 56

– from *Raghuvamsam: The Line of Raghu*,
translated by A.N.D Haksar

'Kumarasambhavam' or The Birth of the War God

Kumarasambhavam, or quite literally, 'the birth or origin of the son' is the second and shorter of Kalidasa's two epics. It describes, in 17 cantos, the events leading up to and the marriage of Shiva and Parvati; the birth of their son, the god of war; his consecration as commander of the celestial forces; and his victory over the daitya Taraka. It relates one of the most ancient stories of humankind, and, through its narration, explores profound and difficult ideas such as the nature of divinity and union with the Absolute.

Despite its subject matter, the epic is not a religious text, but, in the words of Hank Heifetz, 'a secular poem… undoubtedly presented for the entertainment of a king'. The poem, in the recensions available to us today, consists of 17 sargas or cantos. It is regarded by many as an 'uneven' work, in which stanzas of great poetic beauty and power are interspersed with verses that are bland, dull, and undistinguished by any great poetic skill.

Some scholars, such as M.R. Kale, believe that only the first eight cantos are by Kalidasa, and make up the complete poem as intended by him; the remaining nine cantos, in their view, are the work of a later poet or disciple of Kalidasa. Kale points out that while Cantos 1–8 display all the polish, skill, and charm characteristic of Kalidasa's work, the remaining nine cantos are quite unremarkable. The difference in style, believes Kale, proves conclusively that Cantos 9–17 were not written by Kalidasa.

Chandra Rajan, in the introduction to her translation of Kalidasa's poems, suggests another possibility – that the complete epic consists of the 17 cantos available to us today. It may have been composed entirely by Kalidasa, and the uneven quality of the poetry might be entirely his own; or, and this seems more likely, it may have been composed by more than one poet, which more plausibly explains the difference in style and quality between cantos. It is not unusual for Sanskrit texts to be the work of multiple authors – the *Ramayana* is a case in point, as is the *Mahabharata*. Many modern editions of Kalidasa's poem – for instance, those published by the Nirnaya Sagar Press in 1916, and by the Sahitya Akademi in 1962 – treat the epic as a complete poem of 17 cantos. Rajan has also translated it as a poem of 17 cantos, but has kept in mind the possibility that it may be the work of more than one author.

Rajan points out a third possibility – that the epic as we have it is an 'unfinished' poem, the first eight cantos merely a 'fragment' of a larger work (that may or may not have been written but, in either case, is not available to us); and that Cantos 9–17 are 'unauthentic'. Even if we take this view, the 'fragment' of eight cantos is still a legitimate composition, and the epic as a whole with the added nine cantos, worthy of attention.

Regardless of the debate on its authorship, *Kumarasambhavam* is a remarkable work, well-deserving of its place among the greatest of the ancient mahakavyas available to us. Kalidasa's consummate skill as a poet – his luminous language, his evocative imagery, his profound understanding of emotion, particularly love in all its forms, and detailed descriptions of nature – is particularly evident in its initial cantos.

Structure

The title of the poem is made up of two Sanskrit words: *kumara*, which means 'son', 'boy' or 'prince', but is used particularly as an epithet for Skanda, the god of war; and *sambhava*, which means 'birth' or 'origin'. Thus the title may be fully translated as 'the birth or origin of Kumara, the god of war'. As required for a mahakavya, each of its 17 cantos is in a single metre suited to its theme or subject matter. For example, Canto 4, which describes Rati's grief at the loss of her husband, Kama, is composed in a metre called Viyogini, which, in Sanskrit, means 'the woman separated from her lover or husband'. This metre is particularly appropriate for the expression of pathos. Interestingly, as Hank Heifetz points out, this metre, in somewhat macabre fashion, is also called Vaitaliya, 'relating to vetalas', who are ghouls or goblins that haunt burning ghats (with which Shiva is also associated).

Despite the generally perceived lower quality of the poetry in Cantos 9–17, Cantos 14, 16, and 17 give a powerful, vivid, and dramatic account of the march of the celestial army under Kumara, the war that follows, and Kumara's slaying of Taraka.

Summary

Kumarasambhavam is situated in the celestial regions, and all its characters are divine or semi-divine beings. It begins with the story of the marriage of the god Shiva and the goddess Parvati.

Shiva, called the Destroyer, is the great and powerful third deity in the Hindu triad. He balances the powers of Brahma the Creator and Vishnu the Preserver, and together the three keep Creation in equilibrium. Shiva is described as the destructive power, but in Hindu philosophy, dissolution is coupled with regeneration, so as Shiva, he is also the reproductive power that perpetually restores that which has been destroyed. He is also the supreme ascetic, the epitome of penance and abstract meditation through which unlimited powers are acquired and the highest spiritual knowledge is gained. In this form he is represented with matted hair, his body smeared with ashes.

He is a handsome man, though. He wears the crescent moon upon his head, and within his matted locks he holds the River Ganga, which he caught and contained as she descended from heaven upon earth. He has a third eye in the middle of his forehead; the eye, if opened, has great destructive power – it reduces Kama, the god of love, to ashes. He is also the lord of goblins and ghosts – he wears serpents wound around his neck and a necklace of skulls. His steed is an enormous bull called Nandi (who is sometimes represented as his chief attendant and aide-de-camp).

His consort is the goddess Parvati, daughter of Himalaya, king of the mountains. Her name 'Parvati' is a patronymic which means 'daughter of the mountain'. She is also known as 'Uma', which means 'light' or 'splendour'. Kalidasa derives the name from the Sanskrit phrase *u meti* – 'oh do not' – that is, her mother's words beseeching her not to undertake the rigorous penance she is planning in order to win Shiva's heart (Canto 1, Stanza 26). She is also revered as the 'Mother of the World'.

Parvati's mother Mena is also often referred to as Menaka. Her mother is Svadha, daughter of Daksha, mind-born son of Brahma and one of the ten sages from whom humankind has descended. Mena's fathers are the Pitris Agnishwatta and Barhishad. According to the Puranas, the Pitris, or primal fathers, are the sons of the gods; as divine beings they have the power to create offspring only with the power of the mind. Through Agnishwatta and Barhishad, Svadha had two daughters, Mena and Dharini. Mena marries Himalaya, and bears his daughter Parvati.

Skanda or Kumara, the god of war, is the self-begotten son of Shiva. His birth is miraculous, as is fitting for a great hero, and, like many great heroes in myth and epic, he grows to full manhood in the space of only a few days. His victory over the demon forces is never in doubt.

Taraka, Indra's foe, is a daitya, a race hostile to the gods. He is also referred to as an asura in the epic, the closest translation of which in English is 'demon'. In Indra's eyes he is evil personified, an asura who has taken his throne and laid waste his heavenly kingdom. But he is a mighty warrior and a great king, as glorious as Indra if not more so. Moreover, as Brahma points out, he is capable of penance so intense that its power can burn the three worlds. Though the story is told from the perspective of the gods, Kalidasa does not let us entirely forget Taraka's greatness. His end is a warrior's end, one that shakes the world and leaves us with more than a twinge of regret at his death.

The story as summarized below includes all 17 cantos of the epic.

The first stanza of each canto introduces the canto's subject. There is no introduction or opening invocation or benediction for the epic as a whole.

Canto 1

Far to the north lie the snow-clad peaks and forested slopes of Himalaya's kingdom. It is a world between heaven and earth, the abode of sages, siddhas, apsaras, kinnaras, and other divine and semi-divine beings, where hunters and forest-dwellers wander with their wives and lovers. Amid the pine, birch and cedar trees that grow upon its slopes roam elephants, lions, and white-tailed deer, and upon its highest summits lie clear lakes covered with lotuses. The mountain stands, firm and resolute, between the eastern and western oceans, its lofty peaks piercing the sky. He is both the celestial realm, and, personified, its lord imbued with divinity.

Himalaya marries Mena, mind-born daughter of the Pitris. In due course, Mena gives birth to their son, the mountain Mainaka, who, when Indra clipped the wings of the mountains, hides in the ocean and so escapes his wrath. She also gives birth to a daughter, Parvati, who, in her former birth, was Siva's consort, Sati, the daughter of Daksha.

Parvati is her father's favourite child. She is brought up with much love and care by her parents, and grows up into a radiantly beautiful young woman. The divine sage Narada, on a visit to her father Himalaya, foretells that she will become Shiva's bride. Abiding by this prophecy, Himalaya makes no effort to seek a bridegroom for his daughter. Nor does he dare approach Shiva, who, after the loss of his wife Sati, has lost all interest in the world and, retiring to a Himalayan peak, has immersed himself in penance.

Instead, Himalaya directs his daughter, accompanied by two companions, to serve the god and wait upon him in homage. Shiva does not turn Parvati away, and the young woman waits upon him day after day, gathering flowers for his daily worship, cleaning the altar, and bringing water and sacred kusha grass for the performance of sacred rites. She never grows tired, for the rays of the crescent moon upon Shiva's head take away all her fatigue.

Canto 2

Meanwhile, the gods in heaven are in deep distress. The daitya Taraka had, in his youth, performed rigorous penance and received a boon from Brahma that only a son of Shiva could kill him. As a result, he has become immensely powerful, subjugating the gods and making himself lord of all the three worlds – the heaven, the earth, and the netherworld. The gods are powerless to stop him. The Sun and the Moon wait upon him, as do the Wind and the Seasons. Even mighty Indra is afraid to offend him.

In deep despair, the gods decide to appeal to Brahma for help and go to him in a group. Brahma hears them out but cannot help them. Since he is the one to have given the boon to Taraka, he cannot be the one to destroy him. The only one who can stop the great daitya warrior, says Brahma, is a son of Shiva. But Shiva has no son, so it is up to the gods to somehow contrive his birth. Parvati, says Brahma, is the only maiden suitable to marry Shiva, and if the gods can bring about their marriage, they will get the champion they need. So saying, Brahma vanishes.

The gods return to their realm, and decide to enlist the help of Kama, the god of love, in bringing about the union of Shiva and Parvati. Indra travels to Kama through the mind, the speed of his approach doubled by his eagerness.

Canto 3

The god of love waits upon Indra with folded hands. The king of the gods explains the need for a son born of Shiva to lead the celestial army against the asura Taraka. Indra commands Kama to make Shiva fall in love with Parvati, who, at her father's bidding, serves the ascetic god upon a Himalayan mountain peak.

Kama accepts the mission and leaves, full of apprehension, for Shiva's Himalayan retreat. He is armed with his bow and his flower-arrows, and accompanied by his wife Rati, rapture personified, as well as his friend and helper Vasanta, the god of spring.

Wherever they go, flowers burst into bloom, soft breezes begin to blow, birds begin to sing, and love infuses the heart of every being. At last, they reach Shiva's frozen retreat, and even that bleak and desolate peak is transformed. But Shiva remains unmoved.

Kama sees the divine ascetic, deep in meditation, and is unnerved by his incandescent glory. He stands there, not knowing what to do, when Parvati appears with her two companions. At the sight of her flawless loveliness, Kama grows hopeful once again. As Parvati approaches Shiva, the ascetic god, too, comes out of his contemplation. Kama seizes the moment and lets fly one of his arrows.

Shiva is distracted by Parvati's presence, but only for an instant; regaining control of his senses at once, he looks around for the cause of the disquiet in his heart and catches sight of Kama. He is furious at Kama's effrontery. Flames burst forth from his third eye and reduce the god of love to ashes. Rati swoons with shock and falls unconscious, and Shiva, wanting nothing to do with women, vanishes with his ghoulish attendants. Parvati is desolate, and her father, Himalaya, frightened by this sudden turn of events, picks her up in his arms and takes her home.

Canto 4

Rati, Kama's wife, recovers from her swoon. She finds herself alone, and on the ground her husband's ashes. She is overwhelmed by grief and mourns her beloved husband long and deeply. Rati's lament is perhaps the most moving passage in the entire epic. She calls upon Vasanta, wondering at his absence and afraid that he, too, may have been reduced to ashes by Shiva's wrath. But Vasanta, hearing her piteous cries, appears at her side. She asks him to make ready a funeral pyre for her, so that she may be reunited with Kama again. As she readies herself to die, a voice from the sky calls out that her separation from her husband is only temporary; for when Shiva weds Parvati, he will find his happiness again and will restore Kama to his bodily form.

Canto 5

Meanwhile, Parvati is shaken by Kama's end. She longs to win Shiva's love, and after Kama's failure, can think of no other way to do so except through severe penance. Her mother, Mena, tries to dissuade her from such a harsh and difficult course, but her father, Himalaya, pleased by her resolve, gives his consent. Parvati removes her ornaments, puts on the bark garment of an ascetic and makes her way to a high mountain peak inhabited only by peacocks. Here she practises the most severe austerities.

One day, a young ascetic comes to her hermitage. He is Shiva in disguise, come to test the strength of her love for him. He is clad in antelope skin and holds the staff of palash wood carried by celibates. He pretends to be ignorant of the reason for Parvati's austerities, but guesses it is all to gain the man she loves. He wonders who that man might be to remain so unmoved by the hardships she is undergoing. Parvati is unable to speak of her love herself, but her friend who had accompanied her to the mountain peak, speaks on her behalf. The ascetic, learning that her penance is all to win Shiva's love, tries to dissuade her from continuing. Parvati, of course, is not to be swayed. The quick and lively debate between Parvati and the ascetic is one of the most celebrated passages in all of Kalidasa's works.

The ascetic argues with her for a long time, pointing out all of Shiva's shortcomings – the snakes coiled around his wrists, his loincloth of elephant hide dripping with blood, his body covered in the ashes of funeral pyres, his face disfigured by the third eye in his forehead… But in Parvati's eyes, the faults the ascetic lists are not faults at all but the very reasons she loves Shiva. Finally, annoyed by the young man's arguments to the point of anger, she declines to engage in further debate and walks away from him – and as she does so, Shiva takes on his own true form and reveals himself to her. He admits that her penance has won him over, declares himself her slave, and sweeps her into his arms.

Canto 6

Parvati asks Shiva to formally ask her father for her hand in marriage. Shiva complies and asks the Seven Sages to present his suit to Himalaya. The sages, together with Vasishtha's wife Arundhati, visit Himalaya in his beautiful capital city Oshadhiprastha. Himalaya receives them with due courtesy and gives his consent to the wedding of his daughter with Shiva. After fixing the date of the wedding, the sages return to Shiva with the good news. Shiva, eager to be united with his beloved, waits impatiently for the wedding day.

Canto 7

The city of Oshadhiprastha is decorated for the wedding of Himalaya's daughter. Its streets are strewn with flowers and lined with flags of Chinese silk, and its golden gates and arches ablaze with celestial splendour. On the wedding day, Parvati is ritually bathed by the women and dressed in bridal attire. On Kailasa, Shiva, adorned as a bridegroom, mounts his magnificent bull; with his retinue of demigods and accompanied by Indra and the other gods, he sets out for Oshadhiprastha. He is received at the gates of the city by Himalaya and his kinsmen, carrying gifts and mounted on elephants.

As he is led into the city with pomp and ceremony, the women of the city run to their windows to catch a glimpse of

the bridegroom and cannot stop admiring his beauty. Parvati and Shiva are married by the royal priest. At the conclusion of the wedding rites, the gods fall at Shiva's feet and ask that he restore Kama to his corporeal form. Shiva, who is no longer angry, consents. The wedding guests leave, and the newly-wed couple retire to their bridal chamber.

Canto 8

Shiva and Parvati are completely taken up with each other and spend all their time in passionate lovemaking. They stay for a month in Himalaya's palace, then take their leave of Parvati's parents. Mounted upon Shiva's wind-swift bull, the lovers visit many places – the mountains Meru and Mandara, the moonlit slopes of Kailasa, the sandalwood-scented groves of the Malaya mountains, the River Ganga, and the Nandana groves. At last, one evening, they come to the Gandhamadana mountain. They watch the sunset, and Shiva describes the splendour of the evening sky to his wife. As the sun sets in a shimmer of gold, twilight follows and then a moonlit night. The guardian deity of the mountain brings them wine to drink, and the lovers spend the night once again immersed in love. Their desire for each other does not abate, and a hundred years go by as though they were a single night.

This canto is regarded as Kalidasa's finest composition, in particular the stanzas describing the sunset and the coming of night on the mountain.

Canto 9

As Shiva and Parvati lie in each other's arms, a pretty little pigeon flies into their pleasure chamber. At first, Shiva watches it with delight, then realizes it is no ordinary bird, but Agni, the god of fire, in disguise. He is furious at the intrusion, and Agni, terrified, resumes his own form. With folded hands and shaking in fear, he tells Shiva of the gods waiting outside and explains that he comes as their messenger. A hundred years have passed, says Agni, during which Shiva has remained inaccessible, caught up in his love for Parvati, but the gods can wait no longer and beseech him to send forth his son so that he may take command of the celestial armies.

Shiva, placated, showers his procreative energy into Agni, even as Parvati, angered by Agni's interruption, flings terrible curses at him. The god of fire leaves their palace, his radiance dimmed, unable to bear the fierce energy of Shiva's seed. Shiva pacifies Parvati, and presently, mounted on Shiva's divine bull, they leave for Kailasa. They make this mighty mountain peak their home, and, waited upon by Shiva's attendants, live together in happiness.

Canto 10

Meanwhile, Agni staggers into Indra's presence. He is in a sorry condition, burnt black, deformed, covered with smoke. Indra, concerned, asks him what has reduced him to such a state. Agni sighs deeply, and then tells Indra of how he had entered Shiva's chamber in the form of a pigeon, narrowly escaped being reduced to ashes by Shiva's fury, and finally come away carrying Shiva's blazing energy within him. He begs Indra to save his life, for he cannot bear the agony of bearing Shiva's potent power anymore.

Indra calms Agni with soothing words and advises him to immerse himself in the waters of the Ganga. That celestial river, says Indra, is Shiva's watery form (born of Himalaya, she is also Shiva's consort); she will take over Shiva's seed from him and bear it herself. Agni does as Indra advises and makes his way to the Ganga. He plunges into the river, and Shiva's energy passes from him into Ganga. Agni is restored to his former self. But the celestial river is now in intense agony as are all the creatures that live in and upon her waters. Ganga bears the pain as well as she can till one day the Krittikas, six celestial sisters or star-goddesses (associated with maternal care in Hindu mythology and identified with the star cluster called the Pleiades in Western astronomy), come to the river to bathe.

As they immerse themselves in her waters, Shiva's seed is transferred from the river into their bodies. The Krittikas stumble out of the water, feeling as though their insides are on fire. They know they cannot contain Shiva's energy, nor the child now growing in their wombs. In desperation, they throw what is in their wombs into a clump of reeds growing by the river and go home. The boy thus born has six faces, and glows as softly as the crescent moon, which Shiva bears on his head. He is Kumara, the god of war. Later in the epic, the poet also refers to him by the matronymic 'Kartikeya', literally, 'born of the Krittikas'.

Canto 11

At the request of the gods, Ganga nurtures the newborn child at her breast; the Krittikas also return to look after him. As Agni, Ganga, and the Krittikas vie with each other to hold him, Parvati and Shiva pass by in their flying chariot. Parvati is filled with maternal love at the sight of the infant and wonders whose child he is. Shiva explains that the child is her own son, the hero the gods have been waiting for, and relates the manner of his birth.

Parvati picks up the infant, barely six days old, and holds him to her breast. The delighted parents Shiva and Parvati take turns to hold the baby. They climb on to their flying chariot, and, with the baby held snugly in Parvati's arms, fly home to Kailasa. Given his divine nature, Kumara is full-grown by the end of the sixth day and has mastered all the weapons of war.

Kumara's birth is greeted with great joy by all the worlds. Only the glory of Taraka, Indra's foe, is threatened.

Canto 12

Indra, together with the other gods, now visits Shiva and Parvati on Kailasa. He is overcome by Shiva's glory and Parvati's dazzling splendour. Shiva greets him courteously and asks the cause of their distress at Taraka's hands. Indra relates the story of Brahma's boon to Taraka, and Brahma's prophecy that a son of Shiva would one day kill the daitya. He asks that Kumara now lead the celestial army against the daityas and, defeating them, bring relief to the gods. Shiva assents and orders his son to go forth and slay the daitya in battle. Kumara willingly and dutifully accepts his father's command. Parvati's heart swells with pride at her valiant son, and Indra and the gods become hopeful once again.

Canto 13

Kumara, attired for war, leaves with the gods for heaven. The gods are hesitant to enter their own realm, but Kumara, unafraid of Taraka and eager for battle, reassures them. They enter heaven with Kumara at their head.

Indra's realm has been laid waste by Taraka's forces. The trees of Nandana, Indra's pleasure garden, are broken and uprooted, the homes and palaces in Amaravati, Indra's capital city, in ruins. Even Indra's palace has not escaped Taraka's wrath – its golden walls are dented by the tusks of war elephants, the inlaid jewels gouged out and taken away.

Kumara is greeted with joy by Brahma, the divine sages and their wives, Indra's consort Sachi, and all the residents of heaven. He also meets Ganga, the celestial river that had once nurtured him. The gods, rejoicing in Kumara's presence, their hearts full of hope once again, consecrate him as the commander-in-chief of the celestial army.

Canto 14

The heavenly army sets off with Kumara, mounted upon his great war-chariot and armed with divine weapons, at its head. Kumara is followed by Indra, mounted upon his elephant, Airavata; then comes Agni, armed with fire, upon an enormous goat; behind Agni comes the god of death upon his gigantic buffalo. Then comes the demon Nairrta, mounted upon a goblin; Varuna, the god of the waters, upon his ferocious crocodile; Vayu, the wind-god, upon a deer; Kubera, the god of wealth, riding upon a man; and the fierce Rudras, manifestations of Shiva, armed with bows and riding upon enormous bulls. The remaining gods, in their flying chariots, bring up the rear. The war drums of the celestial army reverberate through all of space. The rest of the canto is a stirring description of the march of the celestial army.

Canto 15

The daityas, hearing that Indra, with Shiva's son in command of the celestial forces, is on his way to attack them, grow worried and gather in Taraka's capital city. Taraka, who has defeated Indra several times in battle, laughs scornfully at the news of his approach; furious at what he believes to be Indra's effrontery, he orders his generals to prepare for war. Then, mounting a magnificent war-chariot, Taraka rides out to meet the celestial army. The daitya forces follow with a roar as loud as that of several oceans.

A series of bad omens now appears, but Taraka refuses to turn back. A voice from the heavens calls out, telling him to turn back and warning him about Shiva's son, who, though only six days old, will defeat him as surely as the sun defeats the darkness of night. The celestial voice cautions him not to engage with Kumara in battle, but to throw himself upon his mercy. Taraka threatens the celestials, reminding them of the pain he is capable of inflicting with his arrows. At this, the celestial beings run away in terror, followed by Taraka's derisive laughter.

Taraka now commands his charioteer to drive swiftly towards Indra, and soon reaches the celestial forces, as vast as an ocean, drawn up before him, ready for war. The great daitya warrior feels the thrill of battle coursing through his veins. The fiercest warriors in both armies advance to the front. The gods, though, tremble at the sight of the daitya forces. But Kumara reassures them with a glance and the gods find their courage again. The two armies close in battle. They break all the rules of warfare, inflicting death and destruction on each other.

Canto 16

The entire sixteenth canto is a rousing account of the battle between the celestial forces and the armies of the demon daityas. Foot soldiers, cavalry, elephants, and chariots engage in close and bloody combat. Bards weave in and out, singing the praises of the fallen and the great. Arrows fall thick and fast, swords and lances gleam and glitter as vultures circle the skies. Battle cries full of bloodlust fill the air so that even the mighty war elephants are afraid and trumpet wildly in terror. The bodies of warriors lie on the ground, trampled underfoot or dismembered by enemy warriors. Charioteers die while driving their chariots and are attacked again and again by enemy soldiers believing them to be alive. Wounded elephants run amok, mad with fear and pain. Warriors, having killed each other, continue fighting as they enter heaven – now over apsaras! Amid this carnage, Taraka, his eyes bloodshot with rage, his brows twisted in fury, advances towards the dikpalas, the guardians of space.

Canto 17

The dikpalas, chief of whom is Indra, come together to fight the great daitya warrior. But they cannot withstand his arrows, which turn into hissing serpents and bind them in tight coils. They turn and flee to Kumara, a single glance from whom loosens the serpent coils. Taraka directs his charioteer to drive through Indra's forces. Taraka's war-chariot, as enormous as Himalaya and driven with great skill, ploughs through the celestial armies, leaving in its wake crushed and broken bodies; its wheels are caked with bone, blood, and mangled flesh. The armies of the gods scatter in terror, their shrieks and wails even more terrifying than the thunder of Taraka's chariot.

Taraka now challenges Kumara, and Kumara responds in kind. The rest of the canto is taken up by a detailed account of the duel between the mighty daitya and the god of war. After a long, hard fight, Taraka is fatally wounded by Kumara. The ground shakes with the impact of the daitya warrior's fall, and even the serpent Shesha, who holds the Earth upon his many hoods, feels the shock. But the gods are wild with joy, and surround Kumara with endless praise. Indra regains his kingdom and becomes once again the monarch of the realms of light.

This brings the epic to a close.

Inspiration for 'Kumarasambhavam'

The story of the marriage of Shiva and Parvati is an ancient one, its origins lost in the mists of time. Meagre versions of the story are found in the *Brahmapurana* and the *Kalikapurana*; a detailed version, very similar to the story as given in Kalidasa's epic, is contained in the *Shivapurana*. But all available recensions of the *Shivapurana* are later compilations (though probably based on earlier ones) that post-date Kalidasa. It is therefore unlikely that the *Shivapurana* is Kalidasa's source; rather, it is more probable that the compiler of the Purana copied Kalidasa.

As Rajan suggests, Kalidasa's inspiration for *Kumarasambhavam* probably lies in our vast and ancient oral literature with which he was well-acquainted. With the story of the sacred marriage is interwoven the story of the enmity between Indra and Taraka. This hostility, between god and asura, has its roots in another ancient tale, one of the best known in Indian mythology – the tale of the churning of the ocean of milk.

Once, the sage Durvasa cursed Indra that he and all the gods would lose their strength and good fortune. Vishnu directed the gods to churn the cosmic ocean and obtain from it the nectar of immortality, amrita, which, if drunk, would restore their strength. The gods were too weak to accomplish this on their own and asked the asuras for help, which the asuras willingly gave. The ocean was accordingly churned, and the amrita obtained. But when the asuras demanded their share of it, the gods refused and made off with the pot of nectar. This made the asuras permanent enemies of the gods. Kalidasa, with his usual facility, turns these ancient stories into works of art.

Commentaries

Several commentaries are available on *Kumarasambhavam*. The earliest known commentary on the poem is the tenth-century *Panjika* by Vallabhadeva. However, the best-known and most frequently studied commentary is *Sanjivani* by the fourteenth-century critic and commentator Mallinatha Suri.

Translations and Adaptations

Kumarasambhavam is often criticized by modern commentators as coarse or even irreverent for its frank and candid descriptions of the ardent physical love between Shiva and Parvati. At the same time, the cantos that describe their lovemaking also contain some of the greatest poetry ever written. Though it does not enjoy as wide a popularity as some of Kalidasa's other works, the epic fortunately continues to be read and translated.

Recent English translations of *Kumarasambhavam* include Chandra Rajan's under the same title (1997) and Hank Heifetz's *Kumarasambhavam: The Origin of the Young God* (2015). Over the last two hundred years or so, it has also been translated into several Indian languages, including Assamese, Bengali, Gujarati, Hindi, Kannada, Maithili, Malayalam, Marathi, Odia, Tamil, Telugu, and Urdu.

The seventh-century Sanskrit drama *Parvatiparinaya* (Parvati's Marriage) closely follows the plot and story of *Kumarasambhavam*; attributed to Banabhatta, the court poet of the emperor Harsha, it is regarded as an early attempt to adapt Kalidasa's epic into a play.

Kumarasambhavam is also the basis for a 1969 Malayalam film of the same name. The film, directed by P. Subramaniam, starred some of the greatest actors of the era.

A Glimpse into 'Kumarasambhavam'

From Canto 2

The gods approach Brahma to ask for his help in stopping the depredations of Taraka, and sing a hymn of praise to him. This is an excerpt from their hymn.

Before creation, thou art one;
Three, when creation's work is done:
All praise and honour unto thee
In this thy mystic trinity.

Three various forms and functions three
Proclaim thy living majesty;
Thou dost create, and then maintain,
And last, destroyest all again.

Thy slow recurrent day and night
Bring death to all, or living light.
We live beneath thy waking eye;
Thou sleepest, and thy creatures die.

Solid and fluid, great and small,
And light and heavy—Thou art all;
Matter and form are both in thee:
Thy powers are past discovery.

Thou art the objects that unroll
Their drama for the passive soul;
Thou art the soul that views the play
Indifferently, day by day.

Thou art the knower and the known;
Eater and food art thou alone;
The priest and his oblation fair;
The prayerful suppliant and the prayer.

From Canto 2

The gods describe to Brahma how a daitya called Taraka is tormenting the universe, and despite all their efforts to please and appease him, they are helpless against him.

The sun in heaven dare not glow
With undiminished heat, but so
As that the lilies may awake
Which blossom in his pleasure-lake.

The wind blows gently as it can
To serve him as a soothing fan,
And dare not manifest its power,
Lest it should steal a garden flower.

The seasons have forgotten how
To follow one another now;

They simultaneously bring
Him flowers of autumn, summer, spring.

Such adoration makes him worse;
He troubles all the universe:
Kindness inflames a rascal's mind;
He should be recompensed in kind.

And all the means that we have tried
Against the rogue, are brushed aside,
As potent herbs have no avail
When bodily powers begin to fail.

We seek a leader, O our Lord,
To bring him to his just reward—
As saints seek evermore to win
Virtue, to end life's woe and sin—
That he may guide the heavenly host,
And guard us to the uttermost,
And from our foe lead captive back
The victory which still we lack.

From Canto 4

Rati mourns the death of her husband, Kama, burnt to ashes by Shiva's wrath. These are excerpts from her lament.

The wife of Love lay helpless in a swoon,
Till wakened by a fate whose deadliest sting
Was preparation of herself full soon
To taste the youthful widow's sorrowing.

Her opening eyes were fixed with anxious thought
On every spot where he might be, in vain,

Were gladdened nowhere by the sight she sought,
The lover she should never see again.

She rose and cried aloud: 'Dost thou yet live,
Lord of my life?' And at the last she found
Him whom the wrathful god could not forgive,
Her Love, a trace of ashes on the ground.

With breaking heart, with lovely bosom stained
By cold embrace of earth, with flying hair,
She wept and to the forest world complained,
As if the forest in her grief might share.

***

'I loved to hear the name thou gav'st me often
"Heart of my heart." Alas! It was not true,
But lulling phrase, my coming grief to soften:
Else in thy death, my life had ended, too.

'Think not that on the journey thou hast taken
So newly, I should fail to find thy track;
Ah, but the world! The world is quite forsaken,
For life is love; no life, when thee they lack.'

...

'And when he knows thy life is a remembrance,
Thy friend the moon will feel his shining vain,
Will cease to show the world a circle's semblance,
And even in his waxing time, will wane.

Slowly the mango-blossoms are unfolding
On twigs where pink is struggling with the green,
Greeted by koel-birds sweet concert holding—
Thou dead, who makes of flowers an arrow keen?

Or weaves a string of bees with deft invention,
To speed the missile when the bow is bent?
They buzz about me now with kind intention,
And mortify the grief which they lament.

Arise! Assume again thy radiant beauty!
Rebuke the koel-bird, whom nature taught
Such sweet persuasion; she forgets her duty
As messenger to bosoms passion-fraught.

Well I remember, Love, thy suppliant motion,
Thy trembling, quick embrace, the moments blest
By fervent, self-surrendering devotion—
And memories like these deny me rest.'

...

I see thee straighten out thy blossom-arrow,
The bow slung careless on thy breast the while,
Thine eyes in mirthful, sidelong glance grow narrow,
Thy conference with friendly Spring, thy smile.

But where is Spring? Dear friend, whose art could
fashion
The flowery arrow for thee? Has the wrath

Of dreadful Shiva, in excess of passion,
Bade him, too, follow on that fatal path?'

Heart-smitten by the accents of her grief
Like poisoned darts, soothing her fond alarm,
Incarnate Spring appeared, to bring relief
As friendship can, to sore-lamenting Charm.

And at the sight of him, she wept the more,
And often clutched her throat, and beat her breast;
For lamentation finds an open door
In the presence of the friends we love the best.

– from *Kalidasa: Translations of Shakuntala and Other Works* by Arthur W. Ryder

Acknowledgements

Writing a book on Kalidasa had long been a dream of mine. My gratitude therefore, first and foremost, to Vatsala Kaul Banerjee who gave me the opportunity to write this book and provided advice, insights, and expert direction from start to finish. This book would never have been written without her vision and patient support. My thanks, too, to the team at Hachette India.

I would also like to thank Mriga Maithel for her meticulous editing, and Priyanka Pachpande for the lovely cover and illustrations.

My immense and special gratitude to all the commentators and translators, past and present, whose scholarship and research have made Kalidasa available and accessible to us today. In writing this book, I have referred extensively to many of their works, which I have listed in the bibliography. However, any errors or mistakes are mine and only mine.

Finally, and as always, to my long-suffering family and friends, for their encouragement and understanding, my undying gratitude.

Select Bibliography

Books

De, Sushil Kumar. *The Megha-Duta of Kalidasa*. Sahitya Akademi, 1957.

Dowson, John. *A Classical Dictionary of Hindu Mythology and Religion*, 7th impression. Rupa & Co., 1993.

Evison, Gillian. 'The Sanskrit Manuscripts of Sir William Jones'. In *Sir William Jones, 1746–1794: A Commemoration*. Edited by Alexander Murray. Oxford: Oxford University Press, 1998, pp. 132–35.

Kale, M.R., trans. & ed. *The Malavikagnimitra of Kalidasa: With the Commentary—Kumaragirirajya of Katayavema, Considerably Enlarged; Edited with Introduction, Notes, Various Readings and an English Translation*. The Standard Publishing Company, 1918.

Kalidasa. *Raghuvamsam: The Line of Raghu*. Translated by A.N.D. Haksar. Penguin Random House, 2016.

Kale, M.R., trans. & ed. *The Malavikagnimitra of Kalidasa: With the Commentary—Kumaragirirajya of Katayavema, Considerably Enlarged; Edited with Introduction, Notes, Various Readings and an English Translation*. The Standard Publishing Company, 1918.

———. *The Abhijnanasakuntalam of Kalidasa: With the Commentary of Raghvabhatta, Various Readings, Introduction, Literal Translation,*

Exhaustive Notes and Appendices, 10th edition. Delhi: Motilal Banarasidass, 1969.

Rajan, C., trans. *The Complete Works of Kalidasa, Volume One: Poems*. Sahitya Akademi, 2011.

———. *The Complete Works of Kalidasa, Volume Two: Plays*. Sahitya Akademi, 2010.

Stoler, Barbara Miller, ed. *The Theater of Memory: The Plays of Kalidasa*. Columbia University Press, 1984.

(Comprehensive analyses and new translations of Kalidasa's three extant plays: *Sakuntala and the Ring of Recollection* (trans. Barbara Stoler Miller), *Urvasi Won by Valour* (trans. David Gitomer), and *Malavika and Agnimitra* (trans. Edwin Gerow).

Thapar, Romila. *The Penguin History of Early India: From the Origins to AD 1300*. Penguin Books, 2003.

Books consulted in an electronic format

Ayyar, S. Seshadri. *The Malavikagnimitra of Kalidasa: With the Commentary of Katayavema and Several Others*. Dhyan Prakash Press, 1896. https://archive.org/details/in.ernet.dli.2015.487095/mode/2up (PDF).

Baumer, Rachel Van M., and J.R. Brandon, eds. *Sanskrit Drama in Performance*. Honolulu: University Press of Hawaii, 1981. https://archive.org/details/sanskritdramainp00baum/mode/2up?view=theater.

Dutt, Manmatha Nath, trans. *A Prose English Translation of Harivamsha*. Project Gutenberg, 1897. https://www.gutenberg.org/ebooks/61937.

Dwivedi, R.P., ed. Kālidāsa-Granthāvalī: Sa-Rūpāntarapāṭhāntara-Saṃśodhitamūlā. Kasi-Hindu-Visvavidyalayaḥ, 1976. https://archive.org/details/in.gov.ignca.70476/mode/2up (PDF).

Eggeling, Julius, trans. *Satapatha Brahmana Part V (Containing Books XI, XII, XIII, and XIV), According to the Text of the Madhyandina School. 1900.* https://sacred-texts.com/hin/sbr/sbe44/sbe44109.htm.

Ganguli, Kisari Mohan, trans. *The Mahabharata of Krishna-Dwaipayana Vyasa*. 1883–1896. https://sacred-texts.com/hin/m01/index.htm.

Ghosh, Manmohan, trans. *The Natyashastra, ascribed to Bharat Muni*. Calcutta: Asiatic Society of Bengal, 1951. https://archive.org/details/NatyaShastra/natya_shastra_translation_volume_1_-_

bharat_muni/ (PDF). https://archive.org/details/NatyaShastra/natya_shastra_translation_volume_1_-_bharat_muni/ (PDF).

Griffiths, Ralph T.H., trans. *Rigveda*. 1896. https://sacred-texts.com/hin/rigveda/index.htm.

Hultzsch, E. *Kalidasa's Meghaduta. Edited from Manuscripts with the Commentary of Vallabhadeva*. Royal Asiatic Society, 1911. https://archive.org/details/kalidasasmeghadu020591mbp/mode/2up (PDF).

Kale, M.R. *The Vikramorvasiya of Kalidasa: With the Commentary Styled 'Arthaprakasika'*. The Oriental Publishing Company, 1915. https://archive.org/details/dli.ernet.536578/page/n1/mode/2up (PDF).

———. *The Raghuvamsa of Kalidasa: With the Commentary (Sanjivani) of Mallinatha, Cantos I–X; with a Literal Translation into English, Copious Notes in Sanskrit and English and Various Readings*. Gopal Narayen & Co., 1922. https://archive.org/details/raghuvamsaofkali00kliduoft (PDF).

———. *The Meghaduta of Kalidasa: With the Commentary (Sanjivani) of Mallinatha*, 3rd revised edition. D.V. and B.D. Mulgaokar, 1934. https://archive.org/details/in.ernet.dli.2015.367343/page/n1/mode/2up (PDF).

———. *Kalidasa's Kumarasambhava: With the Commentary (Sanjivani) of Mallinatha, Cantos I–VIII*, seventh edition. Motilal Banarsidass, 1981. https://archive.org/details/KumaraSambhavaOfKalidasaM.R.Kale/mode/2up (PDF).

———. *The Ritusamhara of Kalidasa: With a New Commentary by Shastri Vyankatacharya Upadhye*, second edition. Motilal Banarsidass, 1967. https://archive.org/details/kale-the-rtusamhara-of-kalidasa-2nd-ed.-1967 (PDF).

Kalidasa. *Vikramorvashiyam: Quest for Urvashi*. Translated by A.N.D. Haksar. Penguin Random House, 2021. Kindle.

———. *Ritusamharam: A Gathering of Seasons*. Translated by A.N.D. Haksar. Penguin Random House, 2018. Kindle.

———. *Kumarasambhavam: The Origin of the Young God*. Translated by Hank Heifetz. Penguin Books, 2015. Google Books.

———. *Kumarasambhavam: The Origin of the Young God*. Translated by Hank Heifetz. Motilal Banarsidass, 2024. https://archive.org/details/originofyounggod0000kali/page/n7/mode/2up.

Kalla, L.D. *The Birth-Place of Kalidasa: With Notes, References, and Appendices, etc.* Imperial Book Depot Press, 1926. Google Books.

Karmakar, R.D. *The Meghaduta of Kalidasa. Edited with a Complete Translation into English, Introduction, Notes, Appendices and Extracts from the Commentaries of Vallabha, Daksinavarta and Mallinatha,* third edition. Chowkhamba Vidyabhavan, 2009. https://archive.org/details/sktA_meghaduta-of-kalidasa-with-commentaries-of-mallinatha-vallabha-deva-by-r.-d.-kar/mode/2up (PDF).

Mirashi, V.V., and N.R. Navlekar. *Kālidāsa: Date, Life, and Works.* Popular Prakashan, 1969. Google Books.

Pandit, R.S. *Ritusamhara or The Pageant of the Seasons: Translated from the Original Sanskrit Lyrics of Kalidasa.* National Information and Publications Ltd, 1947. https://archive.org/details/in.ernet.dli.2015.52801 (PDF).

Pansikar, Vasudev Lakshman Shastri. *Kumara Sambhava by Kalidasa: With the Commentary (the Sanjivini) of Mallinatha (1–8 Sargas) and of Sitaram (8–17 Sargas).* Nirnaya Sagar Press, 1916. https://archive.org/details/quGx_kumara-sambhava-by-kalidsa-edited-by-vasudev-lakshman-shastri-pansikar-1916-bomb/mode/2up (PDF).

Pathak, K.B. *Kalidasa's Meghaduta or The Cloud-Messenger (as Embodied in the Parsvabhyudaya) with the Commentary of Mallinatha,* 2nd edition. Aryabhushan Press, 1916. https://archive.org/details/kalidasas-meghaduta-skt-eng-kb-pathak-1916 (PDF).

Ryder, Arthur W., trans. *Kalidasa: Translations of Shakuntala and Other Works.* J.M. Dent, 1920. Online Library of Liberty. https://oll.libertyfund.org/titles/ryder-translations-of-shakuntala-and-other-works (PDF).

Somadeva. *Katha Sarit Sagara or Ocean of the Streams of Story.* Translated by C.H. Tawney and J.W. Thomas. The Baptist Mission Press, 1880 (Vol I). https://archive.org/details/in.ernet.dli.2015.55149/mode/2up (PDF).

Tawney, C.H., trans. *The Malavikagnimitra: A Sanskrit Play by Kalidasa.* Thacker, Spink, & Co., 1891. https://archive.org/details/in.ernet.dli.2015.283495 (PDF).

Velankar, H.D., ed. *The Vikramorvasiya of Kalidasa.* Sahitya Akademi, 1961. https://archive.org/details/velankar-the-vikramorvasiya-of-kalidasa-1961 (PDF).

Online Articles

Anderson, Leona. 'The Indian Spring Festival (Vasantotsava): One or Many?' *Annals of the Bhandarkar Oriental Research Institute* 69, no. 1/4 (1988): 63–76. http://www.jstor.org/stable/41693758.

Athavale, R.B. 'Ancient Sanskrit Drama and Music'. *Annals of the Bhandarkar Oriental Research Institute* 45, no. 1/4 (1964): 19–28. http://www.jstor.org/stable/41682440.

Dasgupta, Sibani. 'The Lyric in Sanskrit Literature'. *Bulletin of the Deccan College Research Institute* 20, no. 1/4 (1960): 347–52. http://www.jstor.org/stable/42929754.

De, Sushil Kumar. 'Some Commentators on the Meghaduta'. https://www.wilbourhall.org/sansknet/jyotisha/papers_on_jyothisa/Meghaduta.htm

Dhikale, Sandeep. 'The Critical and Comparative Analysis of Ancient and Modern Thoughts of Sanskrit Scholars on the "Characteristics of Mahakavya"'. *Research Journal of Humanities and Social Sciences* 15(2): 99–108 (July 2024). DOI:10.52711/2321-5828.2024.00015

Doniger, Wendy. 'Self-Impersonation in World Literature'. *The Kenyon Review* 26, no. 2 (2004): 101–25. http://www.jstor.org/stable/4338587.

Figueira, D.M. *Translating the Orient: The Reception of Śākuntala in Nineteenth-Century Europe*. Albany: State University of New York Press (1991). https://www.complete-review.com/reviews/sanskrit/ksakun1a.htm.

Fleet, John F. *Corpus Inscriptionum Indicarum Vol III: Inscriptions of the Early Gupta Kings and Their Successors*. Calcutta: Government of India, Central Publications Branch, 1888. https://archive.org/details/dli.csl.8714 (PDF).

Gandhi, Shanta. 'A Sanskrit Play in Performance: The Vision of Vasavadatta'. In *Sanskrit Drama in Performance*, edited by Rachel Van M. Baumer and J.R. Brandon. Honolulu: The University Press of Hawaii, 1981. https://archive.org/details/sanskritdramainp00baum/mode/2up?view=theater.

Hiebert, Julie Hamper. 'Royal Evenings: Sanskrit Poetry of Queen and Court'. Harvard University ProQuest Dissertations & Theses, 1988. 8901579. https://www.proquest.com/openview/f423d0e38f59635ea78b7dd080f444b2/1?pq-origsite=gscholar&cbl=18750&diss=y.

Hueckstedt, Robert A. 'The Plays of Kalidasa and Their Major Twentieth-Century English Translations'. *Journal of South Asian Literature* 22, no. 1 (1987): 215–29. http://www.jstor.org/stable/40873952.

Janaki, S.S. 'Abhinavagupta's Contribution to Sanskrit Drama Tradition'. *Annals of the Bhandarkar Oriental Research Institute* 68, no. 1/4 (1987): 525–35. http://www.jstor.org/stable/41693343.

Kielhorn, F. 'Aihole Inscription of Pulikesin II; Saka Samvat 556'. *Epigraphia Indica*, VI (1901), pp. 1–12. https://archive.org/details/EpigraphiaIndicaVol6 (PDF).

Lutgendorf, Philip. 'Ram Teri Ganga Maili'. *Philip's Fil-ums*, University of Iowa, South Asian Studies Program. Archived from the original. https://web.archive.org/web/20111228010453/http://www.uiowa.edu/~incinema/RamTeriGM.html.

Majumdar, Rani. 'Lotus in the Works of Kālidāsa'. *XVI World Sanskrit Conference*, Bangkok, 2015. https://www.academia.edu/88527419/Lotus_in_the_Works_of_K%C4% 81lid%C4%81sa.

Mankodi, K.L. 'The Mandasor Silk Weavers' Inscription of 437 CE and the Temples of the Aulikars'. Academia. https://www.academia.edu/11335052/The_Mandasor_Silk_Weavers_Inscription_of_437_CE_and_the_Temples_of_the_Aulikaras (PDF).

Meera, S. 'Samasyaa Pooranam'. *Triveni Journal*, 1927. https://www.wisdomlib.org/history/compilation/triveni-journal/d/doc70302.html.

Mejor, Marek. 'The Oldest Sanskrit Manuscript of Kālidāsa's Meghadūta from 1363 AD'. Section 4. https://www.academia.edu/45573341/The_Oldest_Sanskrit_Manuscript_of_K%C4%81lid%C4%81sa_ver (PDF).

Mishra, Ram Kumar. 'Pushyamitra Sunga and the Buddhists'. *Proceedings of the Indian History Congress* 73 (2012): 50–57. http://www.jstor.org/stable/44156189.

Murty, Rani Sadasiva. 'The Role of Aesthetics in Sanskrit Literary Criticism'. *National Journal of Hindi & Sanskrit Research*, 2016. https://sanskritarticle.com/wp-content/uploads/8-9-Dr-R.S.MURTY_.pdf.

Neelis, Jason. 'Trade Networks in Ancient South Asia'. *Early Buddhist Transmission and Trade Networks: Mobility and Exchange within and Beyond the Northwestern Borderlands of South Asia* (2011): 183–228. Brill. http://www.jstor.org/stable/10.1163/j.ctt1w8h16r.9.

Raghavan, V. 'A Bibliography of Translations of Kalidasa's Works in Indian Languages'. *Indian Literature* 11, no. 1 (1968): 5–35. http://www.jstor.org/stable/23329605.

———. 'Sanskrit Drama: Theory and Performance'. *Comparative Drama* 1, no. 1 (1967): 36–48. http://www.jstor.org/stable/41152424.

———. 'The Aesthetics of Ancient Indian Drama'. *Indian Literature* 1, no. 2 (1958): 67–74. http://www.jstor.org/stable/23329292.

———. 'Sanskrit Drama in Performance'. In *Sanskrit Drama in Performance*, edited by Rachel Van M. Baumer and J.R. Brandon . Honolulu: The University Press of Hawaii, 1981. https://archive.org/details/sanskritdramainp00baum/mode/2up?view=theater.

Ramulu, A., and A. Ramalu. 'The Times of Kalidasa – An Epigraphical Approach'. *Bulletin of the Deccan College Research Institute 51/52* (1991): 655–58. http://www.jstor.org/stable/42930445.

Rocher, R. 'The Career of Rādhākānta Tarkavāgīśa, an Eighteenth-Century Pandit in British Employ'. *Journal of the American Oriental Society 109*, no. 4 (1989): 627–33. https://doi.org/10.2307/604088.

Sharma, Arvind. 'A City in a Khaṇḍakāvya: Ujjain in the Meghadūta of Kālidāsa'. *Journal of South Asian Literature* 25, no. 1 (1990): 127–38. http://www.jstor.org/stable/40873117.

Shihab, N.A. 'Reason for the Curse in Meghaduta.' *National Journal of Hindi & Sanskrit Research* (2020): 1(32): 44–46. https://sanskritarticle.com/wp-content/uploads/13-32-Dr.N.A.Shihab.pdf.

Singal, Ashok K. 'The Indian Luni-Solar Calendar and the Concept of Adhik-Maas (Extra-Month)'. *Planex: Planteray Science and Exploration Programme*, Newsletter (ISSN 2320-7108 Online) Vol. 3, Issue 3, 2013. https://www.prl.res.in/~rajiv/planexnews/oldarticles/Volume%20-3,%20Issue-3.18-23.pdf.

Sundareswaran, N.K. 'Kalidasa's Concept of Dharma'. Sahityasudha, Calicut University, Sanskrit Series No. 39, 2011. https://www.academia.edu/35420177/Kalidasas_Concept_of_Dharma.

Taylor, M. 'Lambs, Lightning, Nakedness and Fire: Polythetic Networks and Literary Elaborations of the Purūravas–Urvaśī Narrative.' In *Visions and Revisions in Sanskrit Narrative: Studies in the Sanskrit Epics and Purāṇas*, edited by R. Balkaran & M. Taylor, first edition, pp. 441–66. ANU Press, 2023. http://www.jstor.org/stable/jj.13167843.25. pp. 3–5.

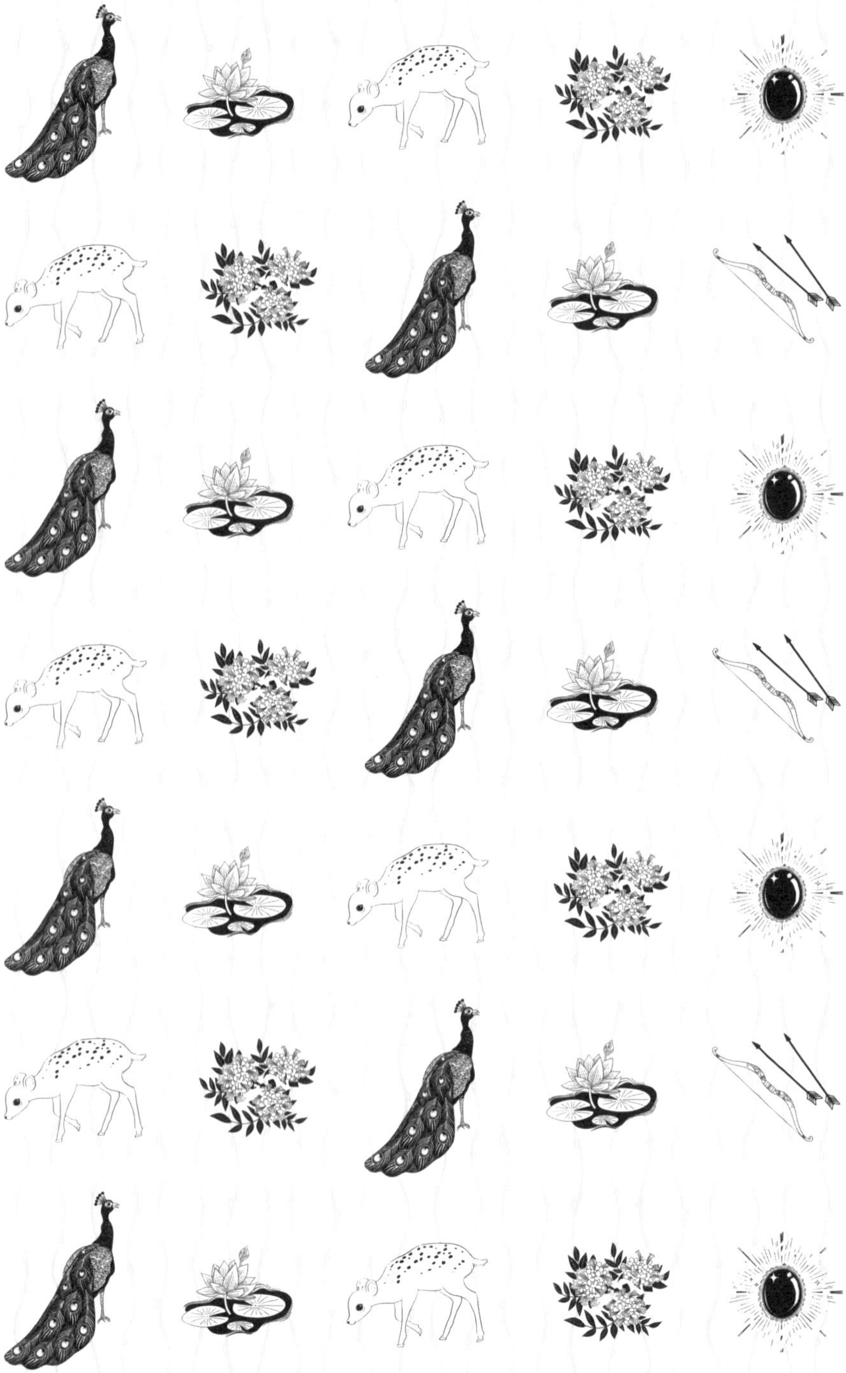